FROM LAND TO MOUTH

FROM

LAND TO MOUTH

UNDERSTANDING
THE FOOD SYSTEM

BREWSTER KNEEN

NC Press Limited
Toronto, 1989

Cover Art: Ricardo Ramirez
Overall Design: Cathleen Kneen

Canadian Cataloguing in Publication Data

Main entry under title:

From land to mouth

Bibliography: p.
Includes index.
ISBN 1-55021-050-5

1. Food supply – Political aspects.   2. Food industry and trade –
Political aspects.   3. Agriculture and state. I. Title.

HD9000.6.K54 1989   338.1'9   C89-093497-5

We would like to thank the Ontario Arts Council and the Canada
Council for their assistance in the production of this book.

New Canada Publications, a division of NC Press Limited,
Box 4010, Station A, Toronto, Ontario, Canada, M5W 1H8.

Distributed in the United States of America by Seven Hills
Books Distributors, 49 Central Ave., Cincinnati, Ohio 45202.

Printed and bound in Canada

ACKNOWLEDGEMENTS

Of all the people whose insights have contributed to the formation of this book, I am particularly grateful to Rose Fugere who provided criticism and encouragement at a crucial moment, and to Louisa Blair, who generously shared her editorial skills. My wife, partner, and critic, Cathleen Kneen, engaged in this project with faith and hard work beyond the call of marriage.

I am also indebted to all of those who have shared experiences, comments, and friendship, including those whose stories are included here under their own names.

The Social Sciences and Humanities Research Council, through its program on *The Human Context of Science and Technology*, provided support for the research and study on the origins and implications of science and technology in the food system, particularly in the dairy sector, which is reflected in this book.

To the memory of "Jiggs" Reardon, my Grade 10 English teacher, who taught me the importance of language and compelled me to think for myself.

CONTENTS

PREFACE

THE FOOD SYSTEM AND ME

In the early 1960s when I lived along the Hudson River in New York State, there were numerous vistas where one could see veritable flotillas of rusting freighters anchored side by side. These retired merchant ships were storing surplus grain. I hardly even wondered about the irrationality of it all in those days. Scavenging discarded fruit in small-town farmers' markets as I hitch-hiked through the U.S.A. in the summertime did not strike me as irrational either. The surplus was taken for granted. If I could make use of what others had picked over, so much the better for me.

Years later, with small children, we were driving through the state of Maine on holiday. We were hungry and came upon what looked like a fair place to eat our picnic lunch. Then we noticed the prolific blueberries, and thought we would try some for dessert. We were quite taken aback by the angry shouts from the woman living next to this field of scrub. Where we came from, blueberries had always been wild "surplus". It was a number of years before I, too, would shout angrily at the trespassers stealing *my* berries in Nova Scotia.

At the age of 24 I went abroad to study. When my money was running out, I was still not ready to return home. I was determined to hold out until I had really sorted out what my convictions were about the world and what were those I had been indoctrinated with as a youth. By the time I did return home I had bald patches in my beard and on my scalp. I had no idea what was wrong with me, and I found out that neither did the medical profession in a fair-sized industrial and university city of New England. I was told to see a psychiatrist, a dermatologist, and so on. With no diagnosis, I went to visit my uncle, a country doctor. It took him about 15 seconds to observe and comment, Malnutrition!

More recently, in Cuba, we were part of a group visiting a small plantation. The farmer was lavish with his samples of oranges, grapefruit, coconuts, and everything else. Most of the group were country people and were at ease with the hospitality. The city girl felt compelled to suggest we take up a collection to pay the farmer. We laughed. The farmer would not have been pleased if we had walked along and helped ourselves, but his pleasure was in sharing the fruit of his labour.

I don't remember ever eating in restaurants as a child, except once or twice a year. It was not my parents' choice for entertainment and later I did not have the money to spend on fancy eating. I do remember banquets, however. At a work camp in Yugoslavia in 1957 I was part of an International Brigade that included a number of Poles. I was the leader of a motley bunch of non-Socialist country youth and, hence, delegate to the celebration of the Polish national day. This was a mid-day feast of Polish salami, fruits, and vodka that the Poles had brought with them for the occasion. I think it was the first feast I had ever attended, and the vulgarity I saw in that celebration made an indelible impression on my Presbyterian consciousness.

Nearly thirty years later we held a feast of our own on our farm. After raising lambs for others for about 12 years we decided it was high time we tried one. So I celebrated my 50th birthday a year early with a whole lamb roasted on a spit, Greek style, with all of our sheep farmer friends and others attending. The next morning all we could find were the scattered bones and empty bottles. I said to myself, "Why did I wait so long to do that?"

It was on my 37th birthday that we took formal title to our farm in Nova Scotia. It was not a going concern at the time. Like me, the fellow we bought it from had not been a farmer, and he seemed to be as short on common sense as he was on financial resources. If I brought anything to the farm, it was common sense, along with my Christian faith, love of Creation, and a sensuous enjoyment of hard physical work. Neither my wife nor I had any farm experience or agricultural training. Some said this was to our advantage.

We moved from Toronto to Nova Scotia as adults seeking greater integrity in our lives and a non-academic understanding of how capitalism functions in the hinterland, the Third World. I knew the theory and when we left Toronto I felt I knew as much as I needed to about how the economy works for the Metropolis. It was how it worked on the hinterland, the other end of the system, that I needed to know.

By the time we left Nova Scotia 15 years later, in 1986, I felt I probably knew more than I really wanted to about the culture of the hinterland. The struggle against the continual drain of human and natural resources to feed the voracious appetite of the Metropolis, its bankers and its elite, had worn me down. Struggling to overcome the fatalism and the opportunism of a colonial culture was equally wearing.

When we moved we did not intend to farm. My aim was simply to get involved in primary production. As it happened we bought a farm, and on that farm were cattle and calves, a semblance of machinery and buildings, and an incredibly beautiful environment. It was July, and the previous owner was starting to make the hay, late. There was little to do but carry on. So we made the hay, such as it was and the machinery would allow, and we put it in the century-old barn, only to discover that the roof leaked badly. So between chasing cattle and repairing fences, with the help of a new neighbour or two I put a new roof on the barn.

Fifteen years later we were still making hay, but we weren't chasing livestock thanks to my border collie partner and our pioneering use of high-power New Zealand electric fencing. We had sold the cattle some years earlier, at the endless bottom of what has been called "the beef cycle", after building up our sheep flock. By the time we left we had built three new barns and improved much of the land. We had even fixed up the house somewhat. We were also working three other old farms.

That first year we tried to learn all we could from books, other farmers, and people like our Ag Rep (Agricultural Representative, or extension agent). Right from the start, with no experience or training, we realized that we would have to sort out the wisdom from the ideology and propaganda. We discovered this when we consulted with our Ag Rep about what we should be growing. His (the Department of Agriculture's) line at that time was "corn". Now, the land we had started to farm was glacial till in central Nova Scotia. We didn't need to be too smart to realize that there were neither the right soil conditions nor enough heat units where we were to even dream of growing corn, except sweet corn in the garden. But corn was "on" that year in the program of the Department of Agriculture. This was the beginning of my questioning of agricultural policy.

During that first year, and every year after that, I learned more about policy and policies in agriculture. I found out that, in common language, "policies" referred essentially to the subsidy programs offered by the government. The total available subsidies constituted policy. That they might have contradictory consequences was less important than the fact that given the level of farm incomes, they were effective in shaping agriculture.

Over time, I came to understand how these policies did make sense from a particular perspective. That perspective is one of the things this book is about. It was not primarily a practical perspective, but an ideological commitment. It reflected the uncritical acceptance of industrialization and concentration, the substitution of capital for labour and the reduction of mixed farming to a specialized aspect of a larger food production system. This included machinery and chemical companies, government advisors and corporate buyers. We farmed during the period when Eugene Whelan, as Minister of Agriculture, helped define farming as one aspect of the "Agri-food" sector.

So we learned about policy as we added up the policies and observed the direction they would take us. We learned about the Market Economy as we tried to sell first our beef and then our lambs at a price that covered both the costs of production and the costs of living very simply.

It was our experience of drovers and agents (who may well have a useful though limited role to play in some situations) and of auction barns and contracts, that led us to intervene on our own behalf in the marketplace, or, in the language of current ideology, to engage in "trade-distorting measures". In the process of organizing a shipment of lambs to an out-of-province buyer, I went to the weekly auction to buy lambs to fill the truck. I made more money off those lambs in one day as a dealer than I could make in a year as a farmer. Reporting on this at the annual meeting of the Sheep Producers Association made me a few enemies and led us into the work of establishing a farmer-owned-and-operated co-operative to market all of our lambs. This opened the door to direct involvement in every aspect of the livestock industry and, indeed, of the food distribution business. As a co-operative, we sold lambs for almost every commercial producer in the province and dealt every day with the region's largest distributor/retailer. We also had to learn about dealing with government regulatory agencies and the business of butchering.

When we sold the farm and moved back to Toronto, we left behind the Northumberland Lamb Marketing Co-operative and the Brookside Abattoir Co-operative, which both continue to function as farmer-owned-and-operated co-operatives. *Northumberlamb*, as it is known, is a non-share capital co-operative, meaning that the structure of the co-operative does not encourage the accumulation of equity or capital. The return to the owners, who are its members, is in the form of the service and price they receive as they utilize the co-op. Thus the refrigerated truck is owned not by the members, but by the co-op as a collective. When we quit farming, we could not endanger the co-op by withdrawing capital from it.

Cathleen and I raised two children, probably the most important crop we grew, on that farm, and when the younger leapfrogged through school so that she was ready to leave home the same year her older brother was, we had to make some hard decisions.

Fifteen years is, in fact, about one generation on the farm. Usually the farm grows with the family, once the kids are on their feet, (literally). When they are 16 or 18, and ready to either leave or take a greater role in the farm, it becomes necessary to make conscious decisions with every member of the family participating. Too often this does not happen, and the story often has an unhappy ending. In our case, it was obvious that our children should go on to university, but by that time we were so involved in organizing and political work that we had become quite dependent on their presence. If we were away at a meeting, or on co-op business, we could count on the kids to do the chores. We had also increased our land base and our flock with their help, and without them we would have to hire help. But the farm could not afford that. Like most farms, we had survived on the basis of the exploitation of family labour, just as happens in the corner store.

We opted for the organizing, the political work, and a new life. We didn't go broke, and because we ignored the advice of all the business advisors and agents, we managed to sell our farm piece by piece and come out of it with enough to move back to Toronto and carry on. In a sense that was the conclusion of a long chapter. When we left Toronto in 1971 we sold our house for what we thought was a good price. We bought the farm, complete with machinery and cattle, for one-third of what we had sold our house for. After 15 years of building up the farm, and reinvesting every penny we ever made, we sold the whole thing for about half the cost of an average Toronto house at that time.

It all added up to a significant learning experience, the sort of experience one does not get in school or from books. It is the desire to share that experience that has produced this book, yet another crop off the farm.

INTRODUCTION

Biting into a freshly picked tomato from a local sustainable system bears little resemblance to the experience of eating a hybrid fruit chemically grown in Mexico with cheap labour and trucked thousands of miles to northern markets in December.

Planting the best seed saved from last years crop, having fertilized the ground with composted manure and other "waste", and planting with it companion crops that will help maintain diversity and resist pests, is the beginning of a sustainable food system. This is not the sort of system this book examines, although the principles of just and sustainable food systems are explored in the last three chapters.

On the other hand, this book is not simply a description of supermarkets and farms, nutrition and starvation, sharing and accumulation. It is a book about *how* the food system functions and how it might function. I refer to this as the *logic* of the food system because I am convinced that it is possible for virtually anyone to grasp this logic, and in so doing to gain tools that can serve to liberate from the fatalism and sense of powerlessness that is so common in Western culture. The logic I refer to can be expressed in the concept of *distancing*: separating people from the sources of their food and nutrition with as many interventions as possible.

The development of this food system need not be ascribed to either ill will or benevolence, but it is, nevertheless, a global, integrated system organized to fulfill a single purpose: to facilitate the accumulation of wealth. Just as it organizes accumulation, it organizes deprivation. With its only ethic that of growth, the Market

Economy of food must continue to extend its frontiers and its logic. This leaves little room for diversity, sustainability, or regional economies. It also reinforces the ideology that there is only one way to organize an economy.

In this book I use the term *food system* to refer to a highly integrated system that includes everything from farm input suppliers to retail outlets, from farmers to consumers. I use it in the singular to reflect the domination of a single world-wide system, although there are still many local, though rapidly disappearing, food systems around the world. The globalization of production, processing and distribution in this system is reflected in the labels in a supermarket, and can be experienced while walking through an ethnic neighbourhood in a large city: our food comes from everywhere in every conceivable form. One shopper told me that of the forty fresh produce items imported from the Third World that she found in one large supermarket, ten came from Chile alone. It is not difficult to find produce from Mexico, Israel or Australia, canned goods from Thailand or the Philippines, or even (if there were labels) beef from Costa Rica or Argentina along with the New Zealand lamb and Danish ham.

The integrated character of the food system, and the characteristics that make it a system, are not so obvious to the untrained eye. The appearance is one of great diversity and many participants, whether as retailers, processors, growers, or wholesalers. There are superstores and corner stores, specialty shops and franchised everythings. On the menu or on the shelf there are hundreds and thousands of choices.

In the countryside there are huge farms and little farms, bankrupt farms and "successful" farms. (It is often hard to tell the difference.) Feed and machinery companies appear under many names (although their numbers are rapidly diminishing), and along with the chemical and seed companies, give the impression that there are many different brands and companies competing in the marketplace.

But the agricultural chemicals will come from one of six or seven transnational corporations that dominate the global chemical industry, and there is increasing likelihood that the seeds will come from the same six or seven companies. (Six seems to be the lowest number for sustainable oligopoly!) The machinery will be an assemblage of globally-sourced components sold under half a dozen different corporate names, none of them Canadian. (Small Massey-Ferguson tractors are made in Japan by a Japanese company and the bigger ones in Britain or Europe. Even as I write this, the old M-F combine plant in Toronto is being turned into high-price condominiums.) The buyers of agricultural commodities may seem legion to the outsider, but chances are that for any single farm product there are between one and four actual buyers.

Appearances notwithstanding, the food system is tightly integrated as a system. There may be many puppets, but there are few puppeteers. It is one thing to count up and describe all the pieces of a system, however, but something quite different to understand its *logic*: how it works and what its rules are, as well as who benefits and who loses. Examining carefully the structures and mechanisms, the logic, of power and control is something we are not often encouraged to do.

Food systems are cultural expressions. The North American food system is dominated by the culture of science and technology which would have us believe that the whole is nothing but the sum of its parts, and that each part, or building block, is a stable, well-defined object that interacts clearly with other objects, through the forces of nature. Such a mechanistic view of reality assumes that once we know how individual building blocks behave, we can determine how a collection of building blocks will behave. It is this view that leads us to believe that a description of the products and the structures, the building blocks, of a food system will provide us with as much understanding of the food system as we can achieve, even though such an understanding leaves us powerless.

An organic food system, however, is not simply composed of a determinate number of static parts. Its components constantly interact with each other and with their environment. A food system, like an organism, can only be understood and described in terms of behaviour, that is, how the parts interact. To try to describe the food system in reductionist, static terms is like trying to describe the process of feeding a growing family by describing the contents of the cupboards and the cooking utensils. Such an exercise might be useful as a way of describing some of the ingredients that make up a domestic food system, but it would hardly explain how the children are persuaded to eat their broccoli.

The logic of our food system owes much to the economic and scientific thinking and social organization of 17th and 18th-century England. Reductionist, linear science coupled with the abstractions of natural law and natural theology were reinforced by Victorian piety and individualism. "The survival of the fittest" as a creed suited well the purposes of those who sought to reduce society to the functioning of a global marketplace, and human community to a federation of classes, a continuing struggle of winners and losers. We deal with this in Chapter 12.

The reduction of food to a commodity and the reduction of persons to consumers and customers are logical expressions of this 19th and now late 20th-century ideology. The unwillingness or inability to imagine or consider alternatives to reductionism is a reflection of the power of determinist science, or "the laws of nature." The passive acceptance by the religious community of the interpretation of God as the great clockmaker in the sky who established the Natural Law and gave His blessing to Science and Economics, as expressions of His Natural Law, imbued reductionism with a credibility that has been as costly for sustainable food systems around the world as it has been for global ecology.

If the objective of a food system were to be the nurturing of human community on a sustainable basis, there would have to be many systems. Each local or regional system would conserve wealth and resources in an equitable fashion and provide adequately for the nutritional needs of every member of its community.

To move beyond this system, to excite our imaginations about the logic of just and sustainable food systems, the logic of *distancing* can be turned inside-out. This yields Proximity, Diversity, and Balance, the characteristics of a different logic which we explore in Chapter 13.

These alternate principles have always been the basis of those food systems that have sustained Native communities, whether in the Arctic, in the mountains of Peru, the deserts of Africa, the rain forests of Central America or the coastlands of the world.

The central celebration of my own Christian faith, a celebration which has long been marginalized as a purely cultic or spiritual exercise, still inspires in me a vision of our possible life together. I experience the Eucharist, or Communion, as a proclamation that there is enough for all if the economy is organized for indefinite sharing, not short-term accumulation. No human community can exist on any other basis. Violence and repression are otherwise required to keep the deprived from taking back what has been taken from them. Human communities are thus destroyed; but community, like food, is essential to life.

CHAPTER 1

THE LANGUAGE OF DISTANCING AND THE PROCESS OF COMMODIFICATION

During the 15 years we farmed in Nova Scotia we grew forage crops and raised beef cattle, sheep, chickens, dogs, and two children. We regarded ourselves as farmers. We never thought of referring to ourselves as "children producers".

People do not normally submit to starvation just because no-one has been around to market some product for them to consume. Eating is one of our most basic urges, and given an adequate income with which to purchase food, or the opportunity to produce it for themselves, people will see to it that they get enough to eat.

In North America, it was not too long ago that every spring farmers would prepare their land to receive the seeds that they had selected as the best from their last year's crop. As the ground was warming, equipment was repaired and the winter's accumulation of manure spread on the land. The farmer did not have to go to the bank, or to the local feed and chemical supplier, to arrange credit and to order the hybrid seed, the agro-toxins, and the fertilizer required for the planting season. The farmer did not need to be a licensed mechanic or a computer buff to get started. The farmer's knowledge, and the secrets of the land being worked, were passed from generation to generation, as oral history and wisdom that could be shared by every member of the community. Farmers planted, tended, and harvested *food*, for themselves and their households. It was stored and prepared at home, without the aid of shrink-wrap and Tetra-Pak, cryovac or micro-wave. The leftovers probably went to the pig or the chickens, without need of a truck to haul away the packaging materials. The jars would be used again next year.

For food to become business it has first to be transformed, at least in our heads, into commodities, because a Market Economy is based on commodity exchange. This means that in our language and thinking we have to separate food from its function of providing nutrition, and turn it instead into a means of making money. Food becomes *product* that has value only insofar as it can be traded in and speculated on. It is logical that we then have to *market* the *product* because it no longer has any intrinsic value to people. "This little piggy goes to market" turns into, "This little product is marketed."

Referring to real live (or dead) pig as product neutralizes it, replacing its use-value with its exchange-value. A food is thus commodified. A pig is transformed by language from something alive that we butcher and eat to some *thing* that is marketed, an object of no intrinsic value and with no intrinsic relationship to life, or to hunger and human need.

Marketing itself is the process of creating a need that can be satisfied only through the purchase of the product being marketed. For example, fast-food industry executives describe their business as market-driven, with the differences between fast-food chains being established not through different products, but through product differentiation achieved by advertising and public relations. McDonald's alone spends some $700-million per year in global advertising, and its outlets in hospitals may be worth more as advertising (the association established between McDonald's and health) than as places to sell food.

Of course, in terms of nutrition, the process of feeding ourselves well is now severely distorted by costly and sophisticated advertising and promotion, which colours our environment and shapes our psyche from birth onwards about what is good, proper and socially acceptable to eat and drink. In 1986, the national print and broadcast media advertising expenditures by food corporations or the food sectors of diversified corporations, (*not* including soft drinks, junk food, household goods, etc.), totalled $235-million. One would have to add to this in-store advertising, coupons and other gimmicks, and various forms of display advertising, from billboards to sports teams.

In the rash of food industry takeovers in 1987 and 1988 (see Chapter 3), to some extent it was brand names that were being bought. Apparently investors feel that the brand names – the labels, such as "Green Giant" or "Kraft" – are worth more than the food they are applied to. The lesser value assigned to generics, or no-name products, attests to the role of advertising and public identity in the food business.

> According to the industry, Canadians spent $1.4-billion for "breakfast products" in 1988. "People are turning to breakfast. By far it is the fastest-growing meal occasion out there."[1]

As language is used to turn food into an object of business, so too is it used to transform farming into commodity production and to alienate a farmer from her or his own labour. For example, farmers frequently talk about "profit" when what they really mean is wages, or "a living". Farmers have been taught by agricultural economists to use the word "profit" for any surplus that remains from the sale of a crop after the cash costs (*excluding* the farmer's labour and any return on investment) have been paid. This, of course, puts the farmer in a very strange position because the labour of the farmer and the farm family is then not considered a cost of production. This obviously misrepresents reality. In corporate accounting "profit" is the surplus *after* all wages, salaries, directors fees, and costs have been paid.

In getting farmers and others to use the word "profit" wrongly, agricultural economists and the ideologues of the Market Economy succeed in their task of convincing farmers and the public that the purpose of producing food is simply to make money, and that if there is anything left to live on after cash costs are paid their farm is "profitable". Of course farmers, along with everyone else, should make a decent living, but being paid fairly for the work one does is vastly different from defining what one does solely in terms of making money, or, in the case of farmers particularly, making a profit. Dairy farmers under supply-management marketing boards are assured, through their cost-of-production pricing formula, of making a decent living – at least in theory – but not a profit. Farmers not under supply management, particularly in hogs or beef, are assured of nothing. Since what they receive for what they produce depends more on market conditions over which they have no control than any amount of good management or hard work they may do, they may receive a windfall profit or they may make nothing.

Market Economy theory also uses the term "competitive", meaning the willingness to sell a product for a price as low as, or lower than, any other seller of the same commodity or product, without regard to the conditions or relations of production. If Haiti is compelled to sell sugar, because it has debts to pay and nothing else to sell for foreign currency, to the Redpath (Tate and Lyle) refinery in Toronto for five or ten cents a pound, utilizing labour to produce it that is paid little or nothing, is that a competitive or an exploitative price (particularly when the cost of producing sugar from beets in Canada is about 22 cents per pound)? In retailing, one often sees prices advertised as "competitive". What is usually meant is that the goods are cheap or low-priced, but these words do not have the moral character of "competitive" in the present political climate.

To be non-competitive is to be immoral in the ideology of the Market Economy. The term is used to manipulate and distract, to keep us from asking why prices for primary products are too low to provide an adequate return to their producers, wherever they might be. It is this gap between the costs of production and the price paid to the farmer that is the major cause of the current crisis in the Canadian rural economy which is commonly called "the farm crisis". Identifying the problem as a "farm crisis" makes it possible for urban residents to remain unaware of the wider social consequences of the exodus of farmers from the land, the consolidation of farms, and the destruction of rural communities.

Government economic advisors call this distortion "structural adjustment" and "rationalization" and it has been an intrinsic and official part of federal agricultural policy since 1969 or earlier.[2]

An Agriculture Canada economist provides a stunning example of the use of language in the process of commodification: labour, including the work of management, is transformed from a human activity into "human capital":

> On economic grounds, justification for government intervention to mitigate adjustment costs is limited. The neo-classical assumption is that gains from adjustment exceed the costs; therefore, intervention is only justified in the event of market failure. One market that may have imperfections is that for human capital.[3]

Similarly, a newspaper article analyzing the 1988 agricultural census reported that "the census shows that 66% of farm women work . . . The women have a variety of occupations." The reporter is not talking about women working on the farm, as they always have, but about women taking off-farm employment. This reflects the same acceptance of commodification: if you do not have a wage or salaried job, you are not working. Work is not defined by what is done, but by its exchange value. Applied to the vast numbers of people, from peasant farmers in the Third World to urban women who raise children and farm kids who do adult work after school, whose labour is either essentially outside a money economy or simply unpaid, it defines a large portion of the world's productive labour as *not work*.

When the farmer and his or her advisors, suppliers, or buyers have come to regard food as a commodity, or a raw material for further processing, then it is easy to apply criteria such as uniformity, durability, and herbicide resistance to its character and production. Criteria such as nutritional value, flavour, and natural disease resistance then become quite secondary, if not irrelevant.

Once food has become only a commodity or a raw material, the notion of adding *value* also becomes reasonable. If the point is to make as much money out of the commodity as possible before it is finally consumed or is thrown out, then it also becomes reasonable to process, transform, and transport the product as much as possible in order to maximize the spread – the profit opportunities

– between the cost of the raw material and the final product on the grocery store shelf.

The less real nutrition in any given product, the more room for profit. Protein is expensive, relative to bulk. The lamb that was compact and firm always weighed more than the rangy "soft" lamb, just as the protein value of the feed could be judged by its weight for bulk. A bale of low-protein hay will weigh considerably less than a bale of leafy alfalfa hay of the same size.

If more wheat can be sold at a lower price if it contains less protein, that is what "the market" (the traders and processors, who work on commission or margin) will demand. High protein bread as a quality food is *not* the goal. Anyway, it is cheaper to add synthetic vitamins later. A senior Cargill Ltd. executive advised an agricultural conference that Canada should be "growing more mid-quality wheat. . . . Our challenge is to grow more tons, value add to more meat, value add again to more further processing."[4] (Just read the label on a package of cheap cookies to see what you might or might not be paying for!)

McDonald's is in the business of selling french fries, not nutrition, so they want "product" (potatoes) that cooks to their specifications, not healthy potatoes with high protein content that provide a high level of nutrition without chemical residues. But it is the consumer who gets blamed for demands and specifications which are actually made by the profit-takers in the food system.

While ground mustard seed has been used in food systems for thousands of years, its use has been limited by the uncontrollable "mouth-heat" it develops. Now a food scientist has developed a way to "de-heat" mustard seed. Since consumers are concerned about chemical additives in food, for example, in processed meat products, it is advantageous to be able to list deheated ground mustard seed on the package as a "spice", although its function is to replace stabilizers and preservatives. "Because of its high protein content (30–40%) deheated ground mustard seed can be used to reduce some of the meat content, thus reducing costs . . ."[5]

Another step in this process of commodification and the reduction of food to raw materials is its further reduction to a "feedstock". This refers not to cattle feed, but to the grain or milk or whatever when it is treated as a raw material for an industrial process that utilizes only certain of its components. In this case, the raw material – what might otherwise be called food – is broken down by one process or another into its constituent parts so that they can then be recombined, or combined with other substances, to form a new desert or a drink, a cereal or a garbage bag. Thus corn can be reduced to proteins and enzymes and starches to become an ingredient in a host of products, which may or may not be edible. Through ultrafiltration, milk can be similarly reduced to a collection of components which can be recombined into whatever product will maximize profit. (Look carefully at the labels on various "dairy products".)

A liquid diet for persons who cannot digest solids will be launched by Nestlé Enterprises Ltd. with the help of a federal repayable contribution of $1,001,300. The diet can be ingested orally or by naso-gastric tube and will be made from Canadian *raw materials* . . .[6] [emphasis added]

Four new products have been added to the Dairyland Products line. Melopro 7500 and Melopro 7600 are isolated wheat protein products that have excellent functional characteristics and perform well as partial or total casein replacers . . . recommended for use in breading batters, diet beverages, meat analogue, and breakfast cereals.[7]

But the reduction of food to a product, commodity, raw material, or feedstock is taken at least one step further. This step we could describe as the vaporization of food, and it occurs when food is transformed into a speculative commodity that can be traded on the futures market. It is "futures" trading because it is trading in a commodity that will only physically exist at some time in the future. Neither the buyer nor the seller can actually touch or own the commodity they are trading because it has yet to be seeded, grown or harvested. (Technically the seed may have actually been planted, but the crop does not yet exist.)

The line between futures trading and metaphysics is very fine, much finer than the line between growing food to eat and buying a contract for pork bellies for next July! But now even the paper on which the contract was once recorded is disappearing, like the crop itself, to be replaced by electronic information that one cannot lay hands on.

For example, the Australian transnational, Elders IXL Ltd., (Foster's beer) which has moved into Canadian beer through the purchase of Carling O'Keefe, is now moving into the Canadian grain market through its subsidiary, Elders Grain. Its corporate promotional material describes its view of what's happening to global grain trading: "Electronic trading of rural produce is developing dramatically . . . With the specifications now used to describe precise qualities of grain, enquiring about, negotiating and closing the deal will soon be possible through electronic screens."

So food, as if by magic, undergoes transformation into "rural product", a raw material, a commodity, or a contract. At the last stage of this profit-production process is the consumer, not as a person, but as a function of the system, making room for more product to be produced and more profit to accrue, as we will see shortly.

The farmer, too, is transformed: first into a consumer of agricultural inputs, then into a producer, and finally into a *businessman*. Farmers are indoctrinated to use this last word in reference to themselves. Obviously the word is sexist; beyond that, the primary work of the farmer is not to do business but to grow food and raise livestock. The farmer who unwittingly allows the use of this term, and uses it in reference to himself or herself, is apt to become alienated from his or her own work or vocation and become instead an object in a system controlled by others. ("Businessman" serves the same purpose as "profit".) The term "half-ton farmer" is used in some places to describe the farmer who spends most of his time running around in his pick-up truck "doing business", that is, buying and selling, making deals.

Renamed "product", food is produced by a businessman, processed, and finally marketed through an outlet (like a field drain emptying into a ditch that carries the water away) to a consumer. Like pig (or pork) being turned into product, persons are turned into consumers, and consumers are only valued if they have the money to become customers. The value of consumers is directly related to their function as a means of getting rid of product, like a Dispose-All, or incinerator. Statistics Canada accounts for this process as the "disappearance" of commodities or food. Given the impossibility of accounting for food in terms of how much is spoiled, eaten, fed to animals, removed in processing, put in the garbage, etc., it is a reasonable accounting procedure, but the irony should not be lost.

The person who cannot become a *consumer* because he/she does not have the money to be a *customer* faces the alternatives of welfare or charity. It then becomes the responsibility of those who do have money to pay their taxes, *and* either donate money to charity or become surrogate customers on behalf of the deprived. Major food distributors like George Weston Ltd. (Loblaws) are high-profile supporters of food banks and food drives. It helps their public image, it helps to keep the product moving, and it helps their balance-sheet if the middle-class can be persuaded to become surrogate customers for the deprived by *buying* processed foods and then, on the far side of the check-out, donating them to the food banks. Better that, than structural changes which would shift or disperse economic and political power. This process also diverts the energy that should be pressing for a change or increase in welfare benefits, and those who get involved in this charitable activity can feel much better about their own life styles than if they were just paying marginally higher taxes.

The reduction of people to functions is an essential premise of a capitalist economy, in the same way that information has to be reduced to a zero-based code to be processed by a computer. Otherwise biological and social considerations such as malnutrition and starvation would introduce "irrational" factors into the system.

We are well along the way of completely separating – *distancing* – human nutrition from the growing of food, interposing vast and expensive industrial processes between human beings and the very simple basis of their existence.

CHAPTER 2

THE BIBLICAL ECONOMY
OF FOOD

In striking contrast to the transformation of food that we have been describing are the stories and visions about food in the Biblical tradition. In both the Hebrew scriptures and the New Testament, and thus for Jews and Christians, food occupies a central place both in the expression of faith and in social organization. My own critique of our current food system, and my vision of other systems, is informed by these stories and their statements about faith and its social consequences.

Christianity offers a powerful and liberating paradigm for a food system, and, perhaps, for an entire economy, in the Eucharist. The Last Supper of Jesus has always been the central liturgical *act* of the Christian faith, however distorted and hidden it may have become at different times.

The Eucharist is the church's celebration of the Feast of the Passover, which Jesus ate with his chosen community: the community that he gathered about him and invested much energy in building. As Jesus shared the Passover meal, the Jewish celebration of liberation from slavery, he turned it into his last official supper with his disciples, a feast that marked the beginning of the end for him. But if it was the beginning of the end, Jesus also recognized the dimension of promise in the words of the Passover service, "Next year in Jerusalem". His followers would not share the Passover again with him, but they would participate in the heavenly banquet, the feast that would mark the beginning of the Kingdom of God, a new era.

The celebration of a key event in the history of the Jewish people took on a present meaning, the celebration of community and shared life, and with it, death. But it also took on the character of promise, becoming a paradigm of hope. The followers of Jesus could look forward to the transformation of the world. The last would be first, the hungry would have enough to eat, and the mighty would be brought low. There would be room for all at the heavenly feast, in the redeemed world.

The Eucharist states unequivocally that God provides enough for all, and all of God's creatures are to share the sustenance of life equitably.

The Passover, however, was only the beginning. After the Jews escaped from slavery in Egypt they got delayed in the wilderness for 40 years enroute to the promised land. They began to panic and complain and to rebel against God as well as against Moses, telling themselves that the slavery of Egypt was to be preferred to the uncertainty, barrenness, and hardship of wilderness, because at least in Egypt they had food to eat. The Exodus story then tells of how God provided Manna for them, so that they would know that "I, Yahweh, am your God":

> . . . in the morning there was a coating of dew all around the camp. When the coating of dew lifted, there on the surface of the desert was a thing delicate, powdery, as fine as hoarfrost on the ground. When they saw this, the sons of Israel said to one another, What is that? not knowing what it was. "That", said Moses to them, "is the bread Yahweh gives you to eat. This is Yahweh's command: everyone must gather enough of it for his needs, one omer a head, according to the number of persons in your families. Each of you will gather for those who share his tent."
>
> The sons of Israel did this. They gathered it, some more, some less. When they measured in an omer what they had gathered, the man who had gathered more had not too much, the man who had gathered less had not too little. Each found he had gathered what he needed.
>
> Moses said to them, "No one must keep any of it for tomorrow". But some would not listen and kept part of it for the following day, and it bred maggots and smelt foul; and Moses was angry with them. Morning by morning they gathered it, each according to his needs. And when the sun grew hot, it melted.[8]

The story does not end there. On the sixth day they gathered twice as much, and when they reported this to Moses, Moses told them that it was all right, that God wanted the seventh day to be a day of complete rest, a Sabbath. They were to eat half of what they gathered on the sixth day and the other half on the Sabbath. To their surprise, the Manna did not rot that time, and there was enough for the Sabbath, but no more.

This story is the paradigm of the just food system, a system in which distancing is excluded by the structure of the system. The very character of the Manna precluded the possibility of speculation. Those entrepreneurs who thought they would gather some extra that they might sell the next day to the shiftless who had not gathered enough got a surprise. Manna, not being a commodity, could not be bought and sold for a profit. Even the Sabbath arrangement left no room for merchants. As food, the Manna spoiled the minute some opportunist thought it could be turned into a commodity in which one could profiteer or speculate. Food, faith, and justice were inextricably bound together.

In the Eucharist, which means literally "thanksgiving", there is always enough bread and wine for everyone present. It would be an unthinkable abomination for the presiding officer to announce part-way through the feast: "Sorry, no more today. Come back next Sunday and we may be able to feed you." Nor does the presiding officer demand payment for the Eucharist.

The Eucharist is a communal act, an act of the community. It is a feast in which all participate, receiving food and drink for the body and the spirit from the hands of their brothers and sisters in the community, in solidarity with those who have gone before, those yet to come, and with all who inhabit God's Creation now. As a paradigm of the banquet in the Kingdom of God, it is a proclamation of how God invites us to live in and with Creation and to organize the economy of our household. This is one of the perspectives from which I view and participate in the food system.

CHAPTER 3

DISTANCING:
THE LOGIC OF
THE FOOD SYSTEM

FROM LAND TO MOUTH

Canadians, like people all around the world, are becoming increasingly separated from their basic food supply. *Distancing* is a useful term to describe the overall effect of the processes that are bringing about profound changes in our food system. In describing those processes, this chapter provides an insight into how technology increases the distance between land and mouth.

Distancing most obviously means increasing the physical distance between the point at which the food is actually grown or raised and the point at which it is consumed; and the extent to which the finished product is removed from its raw state by processing. There was a time when food was grown within the daily experience of just about everybody. Almost every woman was involved in its production and processing (as in Africa today), and it was consumed, more or less, on the spot. To a great extent there was no choice because there was virtually no way to transport food and no means of preserving it in a form that could be transported, except by drying or salting.

The relatively recent invention of the steam engine, the internal combustion engine, and refrigeration, initiated the industrialization of agriculture. (The first boat-load of refrigerated meat arrived in England from Australia in 1879.) Tomatoes could not be hauled thousands of miles overland, or by sea, without both modern refrigeration and modern trucking. The latest stage of this development is, of course, jet aircraft which, because of their speed, have reduced the need for refrigeration, while adding to the costs and making it possible for wealthy markets to be supplied with food grown virtually anywhere in the world. For a price, both seasonality and locality can be circumvented.

Another way to view this is by looking at the production of wheat in Canada. Without the steam-powered threshing machine, the railroad, and then the combine, industrialized wheat monoculture was out of the question, to say nothing of the scale of present grain production. Quite apart from this, the population of the Prairies could never consume anything like all the wheat grown there. Without modern transportation and food preservation techniques, agriculture must remain at a subsistent or self-reliant level. Distance is hardly an issue without technology, and every technological intervention increases distance. The more perishable a commodity is, the more this is true.

The separation of raw food production from the consumers of the final product happens in many ways. The effect of all of them is to increase the distance in the food system:

◻ by physically increasing the distance between where food is grown and where it is consumed;

◻ by urbanizing a population so that it no longer has a rural or farm experience, regardless of physical distance from the land (for example, in 1951 57% of the Canadian population lived in urban (10,000 or more) areas, but by 1981 this had increased to 76%);

◻ by processing and product differentiation which increases the distance between the raw food and the end-product;

◻ by adding preservation techniques and substances so that the time between when the food was alive and when it is consumed is increased;

◻ by packaging technologies that permit longer storage and greater handling and shipping.

In any or all of these ways, people are alienated, or distanced, from the sources of their nutrition. Each act of distancing also introduces an opportunity for taking money out of the system and gaining control over it. Historically, from hunter-gatherers and nomadic tribes to paddy-rice and subsistence farmers, the procurement, preparation and enjoyment of food has been a central cultural activity of human communities. In the industrialized world, however, it is hard to have any sense at all of where our food comes from, how it gets to us, or what happens to it along the way. Rather than being a focal point of our culture, food has become for us a business activity in which we participate as workers, customers, or consumers – and, one must add, owners and corporate shareholders. The experience of having a dinner party in a restaurant may still be an aspect of our culture, but it bears little resemblance to the rural wedding party where practically everything is locally grown and prepared at home.

Until very recently, there were few voices to be heard suggesting that the distancing resulting from the "modernization" of food production, processing, and transportation was not "Progress". Now, however, as the costs of this Progress become evident on farms and in rural communities across Canada and around the world, as this Progress destroys the environment and communities and produces starvation in the Third World, there is an increasing willingness to question the entire system.

DISTANCING IN THE DAIRY INDUSTRY

Modern dairy farms illustrate the development of distancing very well. Before the present technology of dairy farming and milk production, dairy farms and dairies were small and located very close to the consuming population. Less than 40 years ago, fresh milk was still delivered by horse and wagon, as well as by truck, from the farm to a nearby dairy in cans, without refrigeration. The cans were of a size that could be manually handled, and they were not replaced by refrigerated holding tanks on farms (referred to as bulk tanks) until the 1960s. Cows were milked by hand into a bucket until electrification permitted the introduction of the vacuum pump, which was followed in the 1960s by the pipeline milker which could convey the milk from the milking machine directly to the bulk tank without being handled. The milking parlour, which houses all the milking equipment and through which all the cows pass to be milked twice a day, is the latest mechanical-technological development, though many farmers continue to use a pipeline milker in conjunction with tie-stalls for their cows.

But milk tanks required milk tankers; trucks with stainless-steel tanks to haul the milk to the dairy for processing. The introduction of tank-trucks, however, also meant that the distance from the farm to the dairy could be increased since trucks could haul faster and further than horses. Then farmers had to improve their laneways to facilitate the use of trucks, and as the trucks have hauled further and gotten larger the laneways have probably had to be upgraded more than once, thereby influencing the location and layout of new dairy barns and even the abandonment of old ones that were inaccessible to bigger trucks.

Farm mechanization has been accompanied by a consistent trend toward bigger farms and fewer farms. It is generally assumed that this is the inevitable result of Progress; in my view it is neither inevitable nor good. Dairy farms have probably resisted this trend more than other types of farms, at least in Canada, but their numbers have declined and their production and size increased over the years. This has introduced more distancing between farms, and farmers, increasing the difficulty of any kind of co-operative activity. (See Chapter 7.)

As the literal distance between the source of milk on the farm and the consumer in the city has increased – the farms being driven by urbanization and the cost of land further and further from the urban centres – a tug-of-war of sorts has developed between the Milk Marketing Boards and the processors. Since the Milk Marketing Boards are responsible for getting the raw milk from the farm to the processor, they would like the processors to be located as close to the cows as possible, in order to reduce the transport costs incurred by the Boards and, in turn, by the farmers. The processors want just the reverse, preferring to keep their delivery costs as low as possible by locating the processing plants as close to the urban centres as possible. Nowhere is this more visible than in the case of Ault Foods' fluid milk plant, the largest one in Canada, whose five big white raw milk silos are visible to everyone travelling on the Don Valley Parkway in the middle of Metro Toronto. "AULT" on the silos is probably worth more in advertising than the $6.5-million Ault spent on print and broadcast advertising in 1986. (Ault Foods is an operating division of John Labatt Ltd., which is best known for its beer.)[9]

On the consumer side of the dairy, it was common for milk to be delivered daily, unrefrigerated, to the door until the mid-60s. This kept the practical distance between dairy and customer to a minimum, and the traditional intimate relationship to milk as the prime nurturing food was maintained (as in the bedtime glass of warm milk). The disappearance of home delivery was, in part, brought about by homogenization (literally shaking the whole milk until the fat molecules will no longer voluntarily separate as cream), and the universal application of refrigeration: after processing, during transport, and in the home. Now milk is advertised, successfully, as "Cold, Beautiful Milk!"

Refrigeration was only one of the technological innovations that permitted greater distancing of the consumer from the dairy and from the dairy farm. Sterilization (pasteurization) procedures, and just plain cleanliness, from cow to table, account for a lot of the development in this direction, and have contributed significantly to public health.

At the same time, the increasing ingestion of ultra-clean or sterile food probably contributes to the susceptibility of urban people particularly to a host of what are now hostile bugs, bugs to which they were once immune. This may not seem like a significant issue, but when one remembers that the gut is, in fact, a fermenting chamber, dependent for its functioning on a vast army of living micro-organisms permanently resident therein, it is only common sense that the ingestion of dead or sterile food is adding a significant burden to the digestive process, something like trying to start your car in Winnipeg in January without a block heater.

The little coffee creamers and the unrefrigerated milk-based drinks in cardboard cartons are other examples of new technologies which distance in the same way. They have been made possible by the development of a process called UHT (ultra-high-temperature) pasteurization. (Note the "UHT" or "Ultra-pasteurized" or "Long-Life" on the creamer top.) This treatment of the milk to sterilize it is combined with aseptic (sterile) packaging, one of the more exciting and significant new technologies in the food system. (Combibloc and Tetra-Pak are the leading examples of this packaging technology: "The overwhelming popularity of tetra drinks is pushing crystals off the shelves. Tetras used to have a shelf space of two to three linear feet. Today they fill a 12-foot section, six shelves high."[10] The achievement of these combined technologies is that the milk or other dairy product can be kept unrefrigerated for weeks without spoiling, thus facilitating longer and cheaper storage and transport. But this, in turn, makes centralization of production that much easier.

The UHT and aseptic packaging equipment for this process is very expensive and requires a high degree of utilization to rationalize the cost. Of course it also adds considerably to the cost of the product, as does every intervention. The manufacturer of the packaging equipment, the processor who leases it, the corporation that transports it, etc., all have to be paid and they all expect to profit.

Initially there was just one UHT plant in Quebec, and it was capable of handling all the UHT requirements for the entire country. Some of the processors hoped to convince the rest that they should all utilize the one plant to treat the milk that they marketed in the "difficult" (inaccessible) areas of the country where a longer shelf-life was really desireable. It was suggested that each processor could use their own label, and by all using the same plant they could spread the cost of this very expensive technology over the maximum amount of product. This genuine economic rationality did not win out, however, and now all but one of the provinces have under-utilized UHT plants. (There is a contradiction in this, I recognize. Having only one UHT plant would centralize production; on the other hand, centralized processing would have limited the drive to extend the use of the technology.) The cost of this irrationality is, of course, passed along to the consumer.

The dairy processors, to rationalize their investments, also market orange and other juices that utilize the same processing and packaging technology. That is how the dairies got into the juice business, where they now have about 50% of the market. Never mind that when they sell orange juice they are competing with the milk they also market.

The process of distancing occurs everywhere. Vandana Shiva of the Research Foundation for Science, Technology and Natural Resources Policy in Dehradun, India, told me that in her own country:

> The same thing is happening, where distribution is getting hooked up to production and you are distributing over longer distances, and if you distribute over longer distances you must process increasingly. Since you can't transport fresh milk over great distances, you turn it into cheese, but there aren't too many people who can afford to buy cheese. You say you have introduced a new commodity but what you don't say to the people is that in putting milk through processing plants (imported from the West), transporting it over long distances, and producing cheese for the elite, you have deprived the rural person of what milk (nutritional) base there was.
>
> Interestingly, the milk base in the rural areas was there for the poorest person because the way milk was preserved in India was not as milk, but as ghee, or butterfat, which was made out of curd. The buttermilk from the curd was always distributed to the poorest people of the village, it was always available free outside the house of the landlord, so you still had a basic nutrient. The fat was taken away, but all the protein was in that buttermilk. With the making of cheese, buttermilk suddenly disappeared from the scene.[11]

FOOD IRRADIATION

The latest and most disturbing technology that certain interersts are trying to introduce into the food system is gamma irradiation, not because our food, or anybody else's, needs it, but because the manufacturer of the technology, Atomic Energy of Canada Limited, has a technology in need of a market and is trying to justify its existence now that it cannot find any customers for its CANDU nuclear reactors. (The Economic Council of Canada estimates that the federal government has put $12-billion – in 1981 dollars – into development of the Candu reactor, money which is not likely to be recovered.) Like UHT processing, the irradiation of food introduces another cost factor and facilitates greater distancing in the food system. The promoters of the process claim that irradiated food is completely safe and can be stored for long periods of time without deterioration. They claim that this will be a boon to developing countries that need "improved" food storage capability as well as to produce cash crops for export in order to buy food and pay their debts. They neglect to say that the process is very expensive and will further increase the dependency of poor countries on export production in order to repay the loans required to acquire a reactor. In addition food will have to be transported from where it is grown to the location of the irradiator which, because of its cost, will have to serve a very large growing area. For this reason it is likely to have only a negative impact on local nutrition.

A case in point is the irradiation facility being installed in Thailand as an "aid" project financed by the Canadian International Development Agency so that Thailand can grow and export more pineapples. This will cause peasant farmers to stop growing their own food and become wage laborers for a corporation like Del Monte or Dole. AECL has been using this project for its own propaganda, claiming that this technology is wanted and needed by developing countries. AECL is not in the habit of telling the whole story. The day after the 1988 Federal election, AECL Radiochemical, the division of AECL that has been pushing food irradiation, announced that it had changed its name to Nordion, a clear move to obscure the origins of the company and its business interests for the sake of public relations. "Nordion" sounds so clean!

New technologies are continually being developed that serve to increase the distance and corporate concentration in the food system, though they are described as means to providing higher quality and more variety.

PROCESSING AND HEALTHY FOOD

Distancing in the food system means a decline in the real nutritive value of the food as well as an increase in its cost. A freshly picked tomato from the home garden is not the same entity as the one designed and genetically engineered for mechanical harvesting and days and thousands of miles of transportation. Anything picked fresh, and virtually still alive when eaten, is going to be of different nutritive value than something that has been dead or dying for days, or gassed into or out of a coma.

There are many stories of potato farmers refusing to eat the potatoes that they are growing for processing, and eating instead potatoes grown by their neighbors with minimal chemicals on healthier land. The potatoes that McCain's or Carnation wants for processing into frozen french fries are inferior in many respects, not least nutritionally, because they are bred to have certain processing qualities and grown according to certain rules laid down by the processor. Besides the low protein content, such potatoes may not be well suited to the land on which they are grown and may be susceptible to diseases that other varieties are not. They may also be more difficult to store, requiring either costly facilities or high cullage. This is all on top of the problems created by single variety monoculture.

Virtually no commodity on the market today avoids a compromise between the demands of the processor and the quality of the product. For example, when the solids content of a typical tomato is about 5% and the rest is water, with each 1% increase in the solids content saving processors $80-million a year through reduced transport and processing costs, will it be the consumer or the processor that determines the characteristics of the tomato?

The result is a high cost for the final product, but that does not mean the producer necessarily receives a higher price. The higher cost of the product is paid by the land in terms of deteriorating quality, by the producer in terms of deteriorating health due to exposure to toxins of a wide variety and the cost of specialized equipment, and by the consumer who pays for the processing, the transportation, and the spoilage. The consumer also then gets what should be termed an inferior product, very often preserved, coloured and presented with the help of one or many additives. This includes watering the "veggies" in the display case, not to keep them fresh, but to keep them appearing crisp – at the expense of the nutrients. The more dormant a vegetable or fruit is after picking, which means some degree of withering, the better it retains its nutritional value. Watering causes the vegetable to breathe and thus deteriorate, though it also does make the food appear fresher, as fresh as the morning dew!

Not yet on the market is a genetically-engineered tomato which does not wrinkle. A California genetic engineering firm,

Calgene Inc.,[12] in partnership with Campbell Soup Co., has found a way to reverse the *aging* gene of the tomato and then clone the engineered plants. Robert Goodman of Calgene, speaking in Toronto in Dec. 1988, pointed out that, "Many advances have been made over the years in the genetics of the tomato by traditional plant breeding to allow it to be turned into an industrial crop . . . " He then described how 30% of the tomato crop grown on 150,000 acres in the central valley of California is not appropriate for harvesting at the optimal picking time because the tomatoes are either green or rotted and are consequently left in the field.

Calgene came to Campbell's assistance in the search for ways to achieve control of fruit ripening, so that all of the crop would be ready to harvest at the same time, through genetic engineering. Calgene scientists discovered that they could engineer a plant with the polygalacturonase gene turned around backwards, with the result that the phenotype of the plant is actually changed. The result was a tomato that sat on the lab bench for three weeks (Goodman had slides of the tomatoes) and still looked like it had just been picked. Another tomato, without the engineered gene, was wrinkled and sad-looking. As Goodman described them, "These fruits are red, they are ripe, and they appear, by all the tests done so far, to undergo a ripening process very much the same as wild-type plants. So what we have seen is a dramatic extension of the shelf-life of ripe tomato fruits without loss of other characteristics, at least that have so far been tested. Taste has not yet been evaluated."

The first field trial of these new plants was started in Mexico in December, 1988. It was started there because the company had not received permission to conduct the tests in the United States where there is considerable public concern about genetic engineering, and particularly about testing novel organisms outside the confines of a laboratory. The concern is with the potential consequences of novel organisms proliferating in the environment with consequences we cannot possibly forsee. But in January, 1989, the U.S. Government approved field trials of the engineered tomatoes in Hawaii.

While agribusiness in one place is slowing down the aging process of tomatoes, in another it is working in the opposite direction.

Union Carbide, of Bophal fame, markets a plant regulator called *Ethrel*. It is a versatile substance, used on tobacco, cherries, apples, and tomatoes, among other crops. The manufacturers recommend that Ethrel be applied when 5-30% of a tomato crop is pink or red and the rest "mature green". Two to three weeks later the entire crop can be harvested when it is uniformly ripe. What the drug does is cause "an early release of ethylene – nature's ripening agent". There is a problem, however, when this is applied to a crop of tomatoes destined for the retail market rather than processing. Because it speeds up ripening, the tomatoes keep speeding until they rot, which may be the day after you buy them. In this case, the tomatoes are sprayed in order to get them onto the early market when the price is highest.

Another example is wheat as it is grown and wheat as it is consumed, probably thousands of miles away. Up to now, wheat breeding has been successful only with traditional slow methods, and growing wheat is a relatively simple process, with much less interference and imposition than is the case with tomatoes or potatoes. Post-harvest treatment is something else again. Fumigants and fungicides, deterioration due to moisture, and contamination in transport and storage, are just some of the things that affect the grain before it is even milled, to say nothing of what happens during and after milling. (Look at the ingredients on any loaf of factory bread. The wheat was an adequate food when it started out.) In 1986 the United States complained about international competition for wheat sales. Less was said about the complaints from its customers about the wheat they did buy from the U.S.A. regarding contamination and spoilage. The Canadian Wheat Board, to its credit, does ensure a high quality graded wheat for its customers by selling on a graded basis.

Technically, the highly-processed white bread may contain all the nutrients, according to available chemical analysis, of various forms of "health" bread. But chemical analysis does not account for fibre, or texture, and like sociology, makes certain requirements of its samples. It can be argued that the analysis itself alters the substance being analyzed. Whether the human body values all the additives in the same way it would the whole grains is another question, and there are subtleties concerning micro-nutrients about which we still know very little. Interestingly enough, there has been a significant shift in public demand in North America towards more whole grain breads, however that is explained, in spite of higher price.

Quite apart from the question of nutrition is the question of the *structural* effects of new processing technology, such as Washburn's development of an air-separation technique for milling wheat in 1871. This new method enabled the high-protein (high gluten) hard spring wheat that grows well in the dry climate of the Great Plains of North America to be used to produce a pure white flour. This fine flour absorbs more water than the soft (lower gluten) winter wheats of the east, and thus gives bread made with it a longer shelf life.[13] This technological distancing in turn made concentration of the milling industry possible and gave the American millers a global advantage of scale and market reach over the Europeans who were still using the older techniques. (The French *baguette* cannot be made from flour milled by the Washburn technique. That is also why the French buy their bread fresh every day.)

ENERGY INEFFICIENCY

Energy consumption by the food system increases as industrialization and distancing increase. The amount of energy required to produce a calorie of food is constantly increasing, meaning that the system is, by this measure, increasingly *inefficient*. In the early 1970s researchers calculated that "more than ten kilocalories of energy subsidy are now required to produce one kilocalorie of food in the U.S. agricultural-food system", while most non-industrial societies' agricultural sectors are net energy *producers*.[14]

When the cows lived near the people, and the horse that ate the grass along the road could deliver the milk fresh, without refrigeration, the energy consumption of the process was minimal. It is certainly not minimal now, and energy conservation plays little or no role in economic decision-making at the macro-level, although it will be a factor in individual enterprise decision-making. (Efficiency and inclusive cost-accounting are discussed in Chapter 14.)

What this highlights is the fact that our current food system is only efficient according to arbitrary definitions because it is grossly inefficient in terms of energy. There is clearly a direct correlation between energy inefficiency and distancing. Every aspect of distancing demands an energy subsidy, with obvious consequences for people anywhere in the world who do not have the cash wealth to afford these costs.

Let us now turn to distancing where we experience it directly, at the supermarket.

CHAPTER 4

GOING SHOPPING

COVERING UP CORPORATE CONCENTRATION

What we see when we go shopping for groceries depends very much on where we live. Smaller cities and towns present a fairly uniform picture. Where there is no substantial elite of wealth, and the poor are either hidden or desperately attempting to be invisible in the lower middle class, the food distribution system will look very much like that in any number of other similar communities. In a town of 40,000 to 100,000, and even double that number, there will be one or more fast-food strips (very similar to the "golden mile" of new and used car lots and accessory stores one can find on the edge of every North American town and city) with the usual chain and franchise occupants; a handful of convenience stores that are also either small chains, franchises or members of a buying group; possibly a remaining genuine independent; and then the large supermarkets, which range from 40,000 sq. feet to 100,000 sq. feet and carry up to 15,000 different items.

The larger stores will include the very large chains – Safeway, Loblaws (the only truly national chain), Sobeys, Steinbergs, Oshawa Group, Provigo, and A & P (which includes most Dominion stores) – and/or their affiliates, or so-called independents, which are actually members of a buying group under contract to one of the large wholesale/retail chains. Increasingly there is little to distinguish these, as each chain has its flagship stores (the price-setters) which it owns and operates directly; its franchise or affiliate stores that operate under a name such as Mr. Grocer, New

Dominion, Foodland, or Save-easy; and the independents which have a purchasing agreement. For example:

> The Oshawa Group Limited is a Canadian company principally engaged in the marketing of food, general merchandise and pharmaceuticals through a network of distribution centres and retail stores in eight provinces.
>
> Oshawa is Canada's largest supplier of franchised IGA markets, serving 474, as well as many other food outlets and convenience stores. It owns and operates 105 supermarkets of which 51 are Food City, 43 IGA, six Dutch Boy and five others.
>
> General merchandise operations comprise 39 Towers and 10 Bonimart department stores, 50 Drug City and Metro Drug Stores, 22 pharmacies, and 51 restaurants, cafeterias and snack bars.[15]

What you see within these merchandisers of food and other items has changed drastically since the 1950s when every store was uniformly dull and boring, with few concessions to visual attractiveness, and the air filled with engineered Muzak. Not so any more, except for the warehouse or bulk stores located in poorer neighbourhoods. Now the soup cans and breakfast foods are lined up, like the cleaning aids and cookies, in the centre of the store, while around the periphery may be a number of differentiated and apparently independent businesses. In rare cases they actually are. There may be flower shops and drug stores, delis and bakeries, lunch counters and gourmet food shops. The most sophisticated retailers have done away with the music altogether, softened the lighting and added a great deal of visual attractiveness through imaginative use of huge photographs, colour, and space configuration. The crudity of marking prices on every package is being replaced with the sophistication of barcodes and electronic shelf markers. The prices displayed on these miniature radio receivers can be changed from the store office, enabling the marketing experts or the store manager to jiggle prices at will without all the hassle and expense of hiring night workers to change the prices manually. No more new price stickers over old ones, no more consumer observation of the manipulation going on. Price changes can be made at will on old and new stock on the shelf and at the check-out simultaneously.

Apparent diversity in presentation, range of products, packaging, cooking styles, and price, obscures the overall centralizing of control and the distancing. For example, Nestlé (privately owned in Switzerland) makes 200 different blends of its Nescafé brand coffee as one aspect of its diversity in supplying more than 300 brands of food products, emanating from 400 factories around the world, to stores in 160 countries. Nestlé is the world's largest food company with total 1988 sales of $26-billion (US). (Philip Morris, having bought Kraft late in 1988, may surpass Nestlé in 1989. Philip Morris already owned General Foods. The third largest food processor in the world is Unilever of Holland.[16]

In smaller towns there will be limited choice overall, although there may be more variety in a large supermarket that is part of a chain. In larger urban centres there will be not only more choice, there will be differences in what is available in different areas of the city. This will be a reflection of ethnic diversity, but it is also a reflection of the distribution of wealth. In those areas where wealth is concentrated there will be many small shops specializing in one style or type of food, from meat to bakery, deli to fish, as well as a big lush supermarket. This real diversity, which is obvious in certain sections, carries with it a high price tag. In other parts of the city, where there is little excess income, the old shops that used to serve the neighbourhoods are vacant, or house a steady succession of petty shop-keepers with visions of independent success. Most of the money is spent in one of the few accessible large chain stores. Variety and attractiveness are not emphasized, and very often the prices are higher than in a neighbourhood where there is more mobility and experience of choice.

Because of different names, different colours, different labels, it is not immediately apparent that the distribution sector of the food system has been steadily concentrating into fewer and fewer hands. While it may look like there are a lot of retailers in competition with each other, it is more likely that each is functioning according to its alotted role in the system. Competition is very limited, as indicated by the great size and small number of major distributors:

Food distributors in Canada, gross sales:
(last available fiscal year)   *Source: corporate reports*

George Weston (12/87)		$11,034,800,000
which includes: Loblaws	8,630,700,000	
which, in turn, includes		
Kelly Douglas	2,099,736,000	
which, in turn, includes		
Westfair Foods	1,444,453,000	
Provigo (1/88)		6,418,100,000
Steinbergs (7/87)		4,481,664,000
Oshawa Group (1/88)		3,804,015,000
Canada Safeway (12/85: went private in 1986)		3,489,488,000
A & P (2/87)		2,285,939,000
Empire (Sobeys) (4/87)		1,192,902,000

(The buying and selling of groups of stores that occurred with particular frequency in 1987-88, combined with the variety of structural arrangements between wholesalers and retailers, makes any such listing subject to change and error, but the overall picture of concentration and size remains accurate.)

Looked at another way, 56.2% of Canadian food stores sales are by chains (four or more under single ownership) in 1974 supermarkets and 3,924 convenience stores. Another 29.7% of sales are by independents "operating in major or secondary wholesale-sponsored group programs."[17] Given the structure of the sector, this means that the 29.7% must be added to the sales of the 56.2% since the 56.2% are also the wholesalers to the voluntary groups. This means that 85.9% of sales are through the companies indicated above. From this, one could conclude that there is a very high degree of concentration of sales, and control, in the food distribution sector.

Control over the market is also exercised through the practice of the large wholesalers, such as Sobeys or Loblaws, charging different prices to different "customers" for identical goods. Their own flagship stores logically pay the lowest prices, with their smaller chain stores (either corporately owned or franchised) next up the price ladder. Prices go up as the buyers get smaller and more removed from the corporate structure. The percentage differences may be a few per cent to as much as 15% between levels.

The corner store is thus caught in a double-bind. In order to attract customers, it has to provide convenience and variety. That means it has to be open longer hours than the major stores, making it very labour intensive. At the same time it has to charge considerably higher prices than the corporate stores to cover the much higher prices it pays for its goods. There is little chance of a small store growing up into a bigger store in most places.

I refer to the "distribution sector" rather than the "food industry" because the distribution sector does not manufacture, although the distributors are frequently also manufacturers, or own manufacturers or processors. Thus George Weston Ltd., as a food processor, has $1.4-billion of sales, while as a distributor it has $7.8-billion of sales, including its own products. (These figures don't match the earlier figures on sales because they are all approximations based on the limited data available.) Because it is nearly impossible to neatly categorize the corporations as retailers or wholesalers or processors, the entire sector is now referred to in the trade as the PDR (processing, distributing, retailing) sector.[18]

While the operating margins in food distribution may appear low, at 2–3%, the inventory turnover runs 11.8 to 17.5 times per year, providing a return on capital of 12–30%! These figures go far toward explaining the stakes in the game.[19, 20]

Consumer demand and distribution efficiency may seem like cause enough to move the food distribution sector in the direction it is going, but the drive to reduce labour costs is a major factor, as George Fleischman, President of the Grocery Products Manufacturers Association, explained in a speech in 1986:

> The reemergence of smaller non-chain grocery outlets is principally attributed to the new lifestyle adopted by increasing numbers of consumers and the lower labour costs of operating these stores. Most chains operated with organized labour, and union contracts became such a burden, that some chains could no longer maintain their profits. Net margins for supermarket chains run between 1% and 2%; once their profitability was jeopardized, the idea of bailing out of union problems by franchising their retail outlets to independents became very appealing. These same companies in many instances still act as the wholesale suppliers to their franchises or to independent store operators.[21]

In mid-1988 the Steinberg supermarket chain reported that, "The company's 250 restaurants have been grouped into four formats instead of nine: two in junk food and two in healthy food."[22]

DISTANCING BY FRANCHISE

What is happening at the retail end of the system is also happening at the farm end. Farm input suppliers consolidate, so that the farmer, like the retailer, engages in one-stop shopping, buying fertilizer, chemicals, and seeds from one supplier which may be owned by a transnational corporation (TNC) that produces the herbicides and pesticides, the seeds and the fertilizer, like Cargill or Continental Grain.[23] These same corporations engage in biotechnological research with the aim of transforming the seed into a carrier of certain patented genes, which is then coated with the chemicals required to sustain the seed in its infancy until the application of externally supplied life-support products can be undertaken in accordance with the manufacturer's specifications. At harvest time, the purchaser of the resulting "rural product" may be the same corporation that supplied all the inputs, or it may be a processor of that product, whether a meat packer, miller, french-fry manufacturer, canner, or produce distributor who will stipulate the treatments and harvesting dates and methods not already governed by the input supplier.

For example, a potato farmer in Manitoba who sells his potatoes to Carnation (which is owned by Nestlé) gets a lower price for organic, or non-chemical, potatoes because the chemically-grown potatoes *"cook whiter"*. Carnation is *the* french fry supplier for McDonald's in Canada. In the same way, a New Brunswick potato farmer gets a premium from Humpty Dumpty depending on the "whiteness" of the potato he delivers. Another farmer may have a contract with McCain's, in which case the farmer may well purchase fertilizer and seed potatoes from McCains, machinery from McCain's subsidiary, Thomas Equipment, finance his crop through McCain's, and then deliver the crop to McCain's, if they will accept it.

After Cargill Ltd. bought Maple Leaf Mills' grain division in 1988 it issued one of its very few public information pieces. This one was directed at farmers to advise them of the services Cargill was prepared to offer Ontario farmers through its 23 newly-acquired feed mills in south western Ontario:

> Cargill's purpose remains to provide essential goods and services to meet human needs. . . . Cargill offers farmers a complete line of services and crop inputs. Cargill sells herbicides, fertilizers and chemicals, rents out applicators and helps with soil tests. . . We offer farmers a balanced marketing program for their grains. . . . Cargill is a leader in the marketing of farm commodities. . . . Cargill produces top-quality, custom-made and standard rations for livestock and poultry.

Like their counterparts at the other end of the system, Cargill's customers and the *franchised* farmers will be expected to follow directions carefully. What the farmer, like the retail franchisee, will also have to do is to assume the risks that the corporations wish to avoid: the risks of weather, the risks of spoilage and bad temper, the necessity of selling the product when it is ready because it has no value otherwise and cannot be stored, and the problems of labour, whether their own or that of others.

It is often assumed that Canadian agriculture mimics that of the U.S.A. Thus we should expect to find corporate farming taking over in Canada as it has done particularly in the south east and south west of the U.S.A. But our conditions are different, and perhaps the greatest difference, apart from weather, is the lack of a large reserve of cheap labour, such as agribusiness has access to in Mexico or in the large numbers of "undocumented" workers in the U.S.A., i.e., illegal immigrants from the countries south of the border. Canada does use some migrant labour, but on nothing like the scale of the U.S.A. In discussing the prospects for horticultural crop production in Canada, the *Financial Post* commented that, "The main impediment to growth and competitiveness is Canada's dearth of cheap labour."[24]

Agribusiness gets around this labour "problem" by gaining control of every aspect of the food system where labour can be more easily controlled or marginalized than in primary production or some areas of retailing. Thus agribusiness has gained virtually total control over agricultural inputs as well as agricultural outputs, i.e. the processing and distribution of food. The independence of the farm unit is itself illusory. The deed to the farm may carry the farmer's name, but it will be a bank or the Farm Credit Corporation that holds the mortgage. The farmer may buy his inputs in his own name, but they may well be bought on credit supplied either by the dealer or by the purchaser of his production, if they are not already one and the same, (as is often the case in monoculture production like potatoes or cucumbers or tomatoes).

Poultry is the most obvious area of integration in Canada, though hogs in Quebec would vie for the honour. In these cases, the industries are essentially owned by the feed companies who supply not only the chicks (or piglets) and the feed, but also buy the grown birds (or hogs) back for slaughter and processing. What the farmer as an independent operator is left with is the high-risk, relatively labour-intensive area of managing the live birds or pigs. This is virtually identical to the operation of a fast-food franchise, and there are certainly some winners under this system, though there are also losers which we selldom hear about.

Suppliers and buyers at both ends work on a cost-plus basis: that is, the cost of materials, labour, and capital, plus a profit, while the franchisee is strung out between fixed input costs and prices over which he has no control. (In the case of poultry, the supply-management marketing boards do ensure an adequate return to the operator, but the structure is still as described.) The only flexibility or control the franchisee really has is over his own labour or that of others. Given this set-up, there is no reason to expect that corporations dedicated to profit should want to move directly into on-farm food production. Their desire to franchise retailing and concentrate on processing, distribution and wholesaling is based on the same logic.

In 1986, 40% of Canada's retail trade of $44-billion was conducted through franchises and affiliated franchise-type businesses. They employed some 300,000 people. One franchise association estimated that by 1990, 75% of retail trade would be conducted through franchise companies. Genuine diversity will be traded off for uniform variety from coast to coast coupled with centralized control. The Taco Bell in St. John's will be identical to that in Edmonton, and both will contribute to the wealth of Toronto.

Another illustration of the franchise principle can be seen in the area of farm finance. In North America banks and insurance companies and others own huge amounts of farm land, but they do not farm. It is common for a farmer to go bankrupt and have the farm seized by the creditor, who then leases the land back to the same farmer. The creditors know that this is advantageous because no one will work harder than that farmer and exploit his or her own labour more. This practice is reinforced by the creditors knowing that if they put the land on the market, it will depress land prices and thus reduce their equity. So they keep title to the land, as speculators, and lease it out to those who have some commitment to the land.

> The major insurance companies in the United States held over 5-million acres of farmland in 1987. The farms were valued at $2.7-billion and the mortgages valued at $9.2-billion.[25]

> According to the Farm Credit Corporation, total Canadian farm credit outstanding at the end of 1988 was $22.5-billion at an estimated average interest of 11.25%. This includes credit outstanding from banks and other lending agencies, supply companies, etc. Farmers themselves hold about 51% equity in their farms on average across Canada. [26]

Of course, what gets played on at every turn is the image of the farmer as an independent entrepreneur. The franchisee is manipulated in the same fashion: "You've got a great place in a prime location, but business is bad. Your concept is tired, and it's time for a change." So reads an ad for a franchise, but it could be for a farm just as easily as for a restaurant.

A "professional agrologist and consultant" has described the modern farmer this way:

> A farmer is a buyer of land, buildings, machinery, equipment, livestock, semen, quota, feed, minerals, vitamins, hormones and other additives, medicines, seed, fertilizer, insecticides, fungicides, herbicides, small tools, crop insurance, fire insurance, liability insurance, car insurance, workman's compensation, futures, and many other varied items.[27]

The image created by this listing is hardly that of a steward of the land, a tiller of the soil, but it is the image that the agricultural establishment has spent millions to sell to farmers not only in Canada, but around the world.

It is not unreasonable to assert that the farmer is being deliberately alienated from the profession of agri*culture* and recruited to a job and class position that allies the farmer with agribusiness management in the same way that the food retailer and even the consumer become functions of agribusiness. All are supposed to meet the expectations nurtured by agribusiness advertising and promotion. The farmer who cannot command the resources to play the game is dismissed as a "bad manager", while the man or woman who does not command the resources to buy the processed products of the system cannot be a "valued customer".

CHAPTER 5

INDUSTRIAL FOOD

INDUSTRIALIZED LIVESTOCK

At one end of the long windowless barn the 75,000 chicks go in. Halfway along the barn are steel feed bins. Large trucks periodically turn up to blow five or ten tonnes of feed into the bins. The feed is moved by auger and conveyor from there into the barn and onto the chicks' dinner plate. Out the far end, weeks later, come the broilers. On another farm with apparently identical buildings, young hens go in, and out the other end come eggs and, at less frequent intervals, "spent" hens, which go to the soup company for recycling.

To say simply that *industrialization* describes the transformation of farming and the food system in the latter half of the 20th century obscures the fact that ideology and special interests were the driving force of this industrialization. Equated with the notion of Progress, and therefore largely unchallenged, industrialization continues to be a major tool of distancing.

Several processes combined, as they did in other sectors, to bring about the current form of agriculture in North America and Europe: the substitution of capital for labour; the application of the concepts of efficiency and productivity as the key measurements of success; the application of technology in the name of Progress; and the adoption of modern accounting practices, meaning the measurement of the enterprise in terms of cash flow and profit.

The ideology of industrialization *reifies* (from the Latin word for "thing") farming just as it reifies food; that is, both food and farming become *things*, their subsequent value to be determined by The Market, not by whether they husband the land and feed the population. Descriptions of short-term productivity and narrowly conceived efficiency reveal very little about how the farm is really doing or how healthy the children are.

The wholesale application of the type of technology advocated and developed within the social context of reductionist science and the industrial revolution (see Chapter 12) has created tremendous problems for farmers: from the degradation of the land through overuse of chemical fertilizers, pesticides, heavy machinery, monoculture, and cash cropping, to the creation of isolation and stress through the minimalization of labour, and the financial pressure to continually become more "efficient" as a response to factors beyond the farmer's control.

The general public, the consumer, is now expressing some doubts about the whole process and seeking healthier food that is produced under more healthy conditions, from animal rights to oat bran. It is thus essential to understand the bind the farmer has been put in, partly by choice and partly in response to external forces.

The transformation of agriculture into agribusiness occurred slowly and apparently for good purposes. The technological changes brought relief from arduous labour and, to a point, improved the quality of food. Technology applied to food preservation and transportation freed masses of people from rural toil and enabled them to move to the urban centres, where the toil took different forms. It also made possible the concentration of population, industry, and commerce that had been impossible previously because there was no practical way to feed a large urban population. The argument as to whether it was the mechanization of agriculture that pushed people off the farms and into the industrial labour force, or the attraction of urban industrial employment that pulled them off the farms and required the mechanization of agriculture, does not need to be settled here. The results were the same, either way. Agriculture has industrialized at the same pace as the rest of the society. There was nothing unique about the process.

Chicken is cheap, cheap. It is the most highly industrialized meat we consume, and it is cheap at this point because of that. Not only has the production of chickens and eggs been turned into a production line process, the structure of the industry – and in this case the word does apply – itself is industrial, that is, integrated into a tightly-controlled system. From the public standpoint, probably the most important question now is the quality of the product, but the public cannot raise that question without also being willing to consider the question of the price of the product. If one expects or, in the case of the Consumers Association of Canada with its 120,000 subscribers, demands cheap food, then one cannot make contrary demands upon the producer. If the public wants healthy food, that is, food that is health-producing for the consumer, for the producer, and for the natural resources, (whether that be water, land, chickens, etc.), then the price to the producer as well as the consumer must reflect that. For example, chicken will contain antibiotic residues as long as it is produced under the present factory system. Chickens simply cannot survive the stress, to say nothing of the stress-induced diseases, without the antibiotics, which function as tranquilizers. (A different culture might describe sub-therapeutic antibiotics as potions to ward off the evil spirits of industrial food production.)

Late in 1988 in Britain the consumption of eggs and poultry plummeted as a salmonella scare spread. The problem, a good example of *distancing*, is real (though not new) and appears to arise from the high-protein ingredients of chicken feed. Since the whole poultry production process has been centralized and industrialized, from feed production on to the egg or bird for slaughter, it seems that getting rid of the salmonella is virtually impossible. The only real solution is either to literally cook to death all poultry products or to de-industrialize and dismember poultry production. Britain's weekly New Scientist magazine commented in an editorial: "Only a well-coordinated campaign, launched by government simultaneously on several fronts, and with legal clout, can make our factory food safe. The bacteria are not running scared."[28] A scientist at Britain's Public Health Laboratory concluded that salmonella is "the price we pay for the mass production of protein foods."

Animals die when stressed beyond a certain point, and very often this stress is brought about by crowding – intensive housing – which is an essential function of industrialization. For example, on our farm we built a new barn one year, and moved a group of our pregnant ewes into it about three weeks before lambing. They started having abortions, and we had every aborted lamb autopsied by the provincial pathology lab. No cause could be identified, and the cause of death was finally labelled "new barn syndrome" by the pathology lab. (We used to joke about "sudden death syndrome" when hens would keel over and die for no particular reason.) The only unusual thing we had done was to take a certain number of pregnant ewes from an open yard and confine them in a new, totally clean space. We figured out later that we had put about three too many sheep in that space for their emotional and mental tranquility at a crucial point in their pregnancy, although we had followed the space allotment recommended by the textbooks and government manuals. We thought we were being very respectful of their delicate condition. Their abortions were not an expression of disease, but a form of protest at the lack of adequate psychological space.

Modern confinement hog production is very similar. A routine sub-therapeutic (low) level of antibiotic feeding is essential to counter the effects of stress. If the public does not like this use of antibiotics, then it is not enough to demand that the farmer be prohibited from using them. The whole production system will have to be changed, just as it is already changing for poultry in some European countries under public pressure. In the short term costs will increase, costs the public must bear if it chooses to make such demands.

Such a change in the production system will require a prior ideological and philosophical shift away from the notion that we can and must control nature. Yet this is precisely the premise of industrial capitalist agriculture: that we can do what we want and impose our concepts on other species and on our environment with the assurance that any problems created along the way can be repaired with yet another technological fix. Industrial agriculture is based on the premise that we can reconstruct creation according to our ideology with impunity. When chickens die by the thousands when the power goes off and the fans stop running, when pigs start chewing on each other's ears or tails because of over-crowding, or when sheep abort for the same reason, we cannot necessarily fix it with drugs. (There are human analogies, too.)

When the milk from young, high-producing cows undergoes what is called auto-oxidation and develops an "off" taste, the best answer is not necessarily the vet's: large doses of Vitamin E. On the contrary, as one farmer thought about the problem with his own herd he realized that the milk in question was coming from those cows being pushed the hardest. As he thought about the various conditions and circumstances, he was led to suggest to the technicians and veterinarians that the problem did not lie within the cows. Instead he described the milk as "immature", as having been pushed through the cow so fast that the cell structure actually was still immature when the milk came out, with the result that it broke down under stress, that is, when agitated, or exposed to air. Vitamin E might compensate for the problem, but it would not solve it. The solution lay in husbandry and feeding, and in understanding the natural processes at work that have their own rules and limits.

Husbandry and traditional extensive livestock feeding – grazing, use of farm-produced crops, etc. – is a very complex system essentially beyond the control of the purveyors of farm inputs; the drug and chemical companies. Allowing the milk to mature in the cow will provide benefits only to the farmer and the consumer (healthy cows and healthy milk), not to multinational corporations and their sales staff. That the agricultural scientists looked for external solutions to an on-farm problem reflects the current realities of the food system and the domination of reductionist thinking.

Vandana Shiva of India provides a telling description of this ideology applied worldwide, in this case by the World Bank:

> For the World Bank everything works in terms of money. So if there is scarcity, what you do is generate more cash flows and somehow everything will take care of itself. . . . All they see is that there are farmers in Canada and the U.S.A. producing surplus grain, and therefore what you need to do is create some sort of buying power, on the part of other countries, other groups, to sort it all out. . . . there is a way in which you can colonize people,

colonize soils, and translate these into money by over-exploitation, and through that you can colonize the future. What they don't realize is that you can't do the reverse process. You can't have cash flows that will suddenly create soil fertility, money that will bring to life dead streams or bring water to dead wells. They don't realize that nature doesn't get created by money but it can get destroyed for generating money. That is where the logic of the banker is collapsing. They think they can play god, that they can restructure nature, and they think that all the problems of scarcity today, which are problems of the scarcity of nature to produce food and scarcity of humans as part of nature to take care of her needs, are problems that they will be able to solve as bankers through money, cash flows, investments, and returns on investments. [29]

PSEUDO-DIVERSITY

Judging by the 15,000 items that the retailers handle and the wonderful variety of produce that is available now year 'round, one might reasonably think that diversity is actually one of the fruits of the industrial food system. Unfortunately, exactly the reverse is the case, in spite of the apparent variety of fresh foods now available in larger cities.

For example, even though there are 2000 species of potato in the *genus solanum*, all the potatoes grown in the United States, and most of those grown commercially everywhere else, belong to one species, *solanum tuberosum*. Twelve varieties of this one species constitute 85% of the U.S. potato harvest, but the one variety most favoured by the processors, the Russet Burbank, is by far the dominant variety. In 1982, 40% of the potatoes planted in the U.S. were Russet Burbanks.[30]

McDonald's Corporation in Britain is switching from the Pentland Dell variety of potato to the Russet Burbank because, "it is a more suitable potato for our requirements". McDonald's uses 55,000 tons of potatoes a year in Britain.[31]

Other major crops provide similar examples of the narrow genetic base of our food system. Although there are more than 250 varieties of wheat available, in 1981 only six varieties accounted for nearly 40% of United States' wheat acreage while only four varieties of rice accounted for 65% of the rice acreage; six for 42% of the soybean land; three for 76% of the snap beans planted; two for 96% of the peas; and nine for 95% of the peanuts.[32]

In Canada, four varieties of wheat produce 75% of the crop grown on the Prairies and more than half of it comes from a single variety, Neepawa.

Appearances would give us the idea that there is a constantly increasing variety of both raw and processed food in our food system, but the fact of the matter is that the industrialized agriculture of North America has been systematically reducing genetic variety in the food system while increasing the apparent variety of what is referred to in the trade as "product", whether this be in seed corn or corn flakes, strains of wheat or varieties of bread, types of cows or qualities of cheese, potatoes or potato chips. Where once the global food supply was derived from 3–4,000 different crops, we are now dependent on 29 or 30![33]

A reflection of this is found in the declining numbers of small independent seed companies. The Seed Saver Exchange of Iowa has found that out of 230 companies inventoried in 1984, 54 were no longer in business in 1987. In addition, larger companies prefer hybrids and patented seeds because the gardener cannot save seed from these plants for the next year, either because they will not breed true, in the case of hybrids, or because the gardener would have to pay royalties, in the case of patented seed. Thus Seed Saver found that 943 open-pollinated varieties available in 1984 were no longer available from seed companies in 1987.

There is a region in India that today has no food, because a tribal group that lived off forests, on forest herbs and forest tubers and forest produce, who 20 years ago were living on 180 varieties of food from the forest, were called primitive. So you introduced the Green Revolution to teach them rice farming and what you have at the end is collapsed rice farming because it was not ecologically sound, and you have deforested the region and produced famine where there had been none.[34]

UNIFORMITY

Monoculture – the deliberate choice of uniformity and the continuous production of a single crop – appears to be a prerequisite to industrial agriculture. For example, machine harvesting requires harvesting of an entire field, of whatever size, at one time. This means that whatever is in that field must be ready for harvest at the same time and subject to harvesting by a single process, as we have already described with tomatoes. Two kinds of uniformity are thus demanded of a single crop: uniformity in maturity and uniformity in size and shape. Since this is quite unnatural, various agrotoxins often have to be used, such as top-killers and growth regulators, in addition to the breeding, engineering, or selection of the seed for uniformity. Hybrids are attractive because they provide this uniformity along with other attributes (see Chapter 9).

The demand for uniformity prohibits cultural practices like intercropping – the growing of complementary crops in the same field – as well as the spreading of the harvest season so that it is less intensive and thus less demanding on both machinery and labour. Potato production is a good example. Until the harvester was introduced around 1965, thirty acres was about the maximum size of a New Brunswick potato farm. The family could perform the regular seasonal work while relying on additional local labour, school children and others, for the harvest. The schools accommodated this in their scheduling. The harvester, however, required a minimum of eighty acres of potatoes to finance the machine. This increase in farm size in turn required a whole new system of machinery since the family could no longer perform the regular work required to grow that large a crop. This transformation of New Brunswick (and Prince Edward Island) farming brought with it farm closures and farm consolidation as well as a drastic increase in farm capitalization. The social and ecological consequences were equally drastic.[35]

Uniformity in the field is required by the machine that will harvest it, while the size of the field is strongly determined by the size of the machine. The size of the machine is determined both by the functions assigned to it and by the economics of producing the machine. Sugar combines or potato harvesters must be big machines because of what they are required to do, and the fields must be of a certain minimum size to permit even the turning of the machine, to say nothing of its efficient operation.

Mechanized seeding, watering, cultivating, and fertilization also impose their requirements on the production process, but the requirements for uniformity do not end with the harvesting of the raw material. The processing itself requires uniformity, as does the packaging and even the transporting of food.

For example, while the McIntosh apple has been the most popular apple in Ontario for growers and the public since early this century, the Empire is gaining fast. Whether this is because the public prefers it to the Mac may be open to some question. Produce managers want a "12-month" apple that can survive long storage and rough handling. The Mac, discovered by John McIntosh in 1811 as a wild tree and subsequently bred for flavour and keeping qualities into the apple we know so well, is being overtaken by an apple developed by scientists at the New York State Experimental Farm in Geneva, N.Y. in 1966. An apple industry executive said that the industry needs a "hardware-type product" like the Empire in order "to withstand the rigors of today's modern packaging and merchandising techniques".

We encountered the industrial demand for uniformity on our own farm when we tried to seed bromegrass and alfalfa together. (They are excellent companion crops because the alfalfa fixes nitrogen in the ground which the bromegrass utilizes, and they have similar growth patterns.) But bromegrass is a large, light, chaffy seed, while alfalfa is a small, round, heavy seed. It is virtually impossible to seed the two simultaneously except with a piece of expensive, specialized equipment. The alternative is to make two passes over the field. So even though the two are particularly suited as companion crops, the farmer is tempted to settle for some other mixture that can be seeded in one pass for the sake of immediate efficiency or productivity, meaning how much can be done by one person in the shortest possible time. This does not encourage either genetic or practical diversity.

Mechanical uniformity is only one expression of the uniformity sought and demanded in the food system. One established means of achieving uniformity, and greatly increasing the distance in the food system, is through hybridization. This is a process of selective breeding through traditional practices, or now through genetic manipulation, that produces a plant or even an animal that is incapable of breeding true, or in some cases, breeding at all. Seedless mandarin oranges, the hundreds of corn hybrids, many ornamental plants and flowers, as well as strawberry plants and mules all share this common character: they are evolutionary misfits, incapable of reproducing themselves. Insofar as we build our food system upon them, our food system is similarly dependent on the designers, inventors, and technicians who reproduce these plants and animals, and the corporations that employ them.

Hybridization produces uniformity with a vengeance, as well as being "the prime mover for the industrial appropriation of the natural production process."[36] Thus the world's largest grain trading corporation, Cargill, is hard at work engineering hybrid Canola plants as well as corn and sorghum, and university labs in Canada and the U.S.A. are busy seeking industrial support for their work in plant and animal cloning and other techniques of producing totally uniform living machines for the production of food as well as non-food commodities as the raw material for the processing industries. The result is the *trivializing* of agriculture,[37] transforming agriculture into a parts manufacturer. Fast approaching is the day when our food will be assembled much like an industrial product, with the components, or parts, being "sourced" from whatever supplier will produce them most cheaply, anywhere in the world. The sources may be low-wage growing areas, states with minimum ecological protection legislation and enforcement, or protein or starch factories located next to the major markets for food products.[38]

CHAPTER 6

STORIES FROM
THE LAND

While Cathleen and I were farming we
started publishing *The Ram's Horn* as a
newsletter for sheep farmers. It gradually
broadened in scope and readership. Over the
years we have published some stories from
other farmers as well as our own. These are
a few of them, the "photo album" for this
book.

ON BLUEBERRY HILL
JOHN MILDON
Upper Stewiacke, Nova Scotia

Every year, about this time, the notices go up in our local Co-Op inviting the young people of the community to sign up to rake blueberries. During the dog days of August, it is the last ritual of summer before the school year begins again.

Throughout the province, the scramble will be on to harvest Nova Scotia's richest export fruit. Mobs of kids in sneakers, bright coloured T-shirts and jeans will bend over in the hot sun, rake in hand, and straggle out along lines of string on the barrens to gather the berries which contributed $16 million to the economy last year.

If progress has its way these same kids will soon be kicking stones on street corners along with all the other students who have vainly looked for work to help pay their school bills, or augment their pocket money. This year, for the first time, 22 mechanical harvesters constructed by Bragg Lumber in Collingwood will be operating throughout the province. If they work as well as expected, there will be more and eventually hand raking will be a thing of the past.

There are those who will argue that is good. To force youngsters to work in the heat and race to fill their buckets for minimal wages is exploitation of labour at its worst. Many growers will be relieved. Young labour is a headache: crews to be organized, picked up, taken home, paid. Some of them goof off, trample more than they rake, distract their friends, fall sick, or want the bathroom. Machines are far better.

Or, you can look at it this way: blueberries are a useful little cash crop for many farmers. The harvest is almost a family affair. The kids are mostly their own, or their neighbours'. The youngsters know each other. Most of them want to rake willingly and with enthusiasm. It is a sport as much as a job. It is a challenge, a contest of stamina, speed, dexterity. Boys and girls vie with their best friends. The girls try to outstrip the boys in adolescent, asexual competition. At the end of it, the dollars in the pocket reflect accomplishment, encourage independence and self-reliance.

The mechanical harvester will change that. Smaller growers will not be able to afford the capital investment. They will continue to hand rake until it is no longer competitive. Then their best acreages will be sold off or leased to someone with a machine. The marginal land will revert to bush. Machines, unlike kids, can only harvest the larger, more open and flatter fields.

The use of herbicides to kill competition, and fertilizer to increase yields, will increase to make the machine more cost-effective.

A larger share of the grower's dollar will be spent on materials and machinery from outside the community.

The kids will put their energy into defacing the post office, or kicking in the windows of the gas station and store.

It's a shame about the blueberry festival. That string of Bragg harvesters proceeding through the village is not as pretty a sight as the parade of floats done up by the growers and their picking crews that we used to see hereabouts.

And you can't blame the womenfolk for serving up those McCain's frozen blueberry pies, but do you remember those plates of fresh homemade blueberry muffins, grunt, tarts, and the jams and preserves?

I'm not against progress. It's against me.

from *The Ram's Horn*, August 1984

FARMERS AS EXPLOITERS

from a conversation with
DARRELL McLAUGHLIN
Aroostook, New Brunswick

On the other hand, we need to also be aware of farmers as exploiters. The desperation to maintain the "lifestyle", the tradition, the family heritage, results in exploitation of: first, the wife, through overwork and isolation; then, the children, with the statement that they will receive just what the rest of the family receives (that is, food and lodging); and then of course the land and animals are exploited; and then the employees. I am aware of a tendency to pad my living at the expense of the people I employ: around me I see workers making up the difference between viable and non-viable farms; wage-labourers replace farmers; UIC and welfare payments replace subsidies to farmers. If you add up New Brunswick's total potato production and divide it by the man-hours of work of farmers and wage-labourers, you come up with the figure that at present, 60% of the potatoes produced in New Brunswick are produced by wage labour.

You have to remember that the Maritimes' tradition is rural; the people who settled here came themselves from a rural background. But at this time, with the change in society and the availability of work in town or country, it seems to me that the people who continue to live in the isolated rural areas are casualties, victims, or refugees of our advancing society.

Growth: if you go for a 50-100 hp tractor you have to farm your neighbour's land. And it is outside forces that are designing this technology; it is not coming from the farmers, who are poorly organized and therefore unable to describe their technological needs in a powerful way. One should also recognize that, for example, the 15-bottom plow takes *more*, not less, time, and requires more production. It's clear that the reason for this technology is not really to make life easier for the farmer, but to change the nature of farming. It has changed the inter-dependence of rural communities to raw dependency.

Without getting romantic about it, I think we can talk about the sense of satisfaction farmers get from working. There isn't anything quite like the feeling when after pushing yourselves harder than you thought you could, the job is finally done. In the potatoes area, when the potatoes are all in the potato house and you say to yourself, well, we did it. I think what has given life to farmers is producing. But now some farmers are working just to be consumers, whether it's bigger cars, tractors and trucks or CBs or whatever. I see a huge change from working to produce, to working to consume.

from *The Ram's Horn*, June, 1984

CROP FAILURE
BREWSTER and CATHLEEN KNEEN
Brookland, Pictou Co., Nova Scotia

It took a trip out West, listening to Prairie farmers talk about the drought and the threat of grasshoppers, to make us realize that as livestock farmers we also face crop failures. When it doesn't rain and the crop doesn't grow, that's clearly an "act of God" about which we can do nothing but shrug our shoulders and, as farmers have for centuries, hope for a better year next year. That's what we usually think of as crop failure. In livestock it does sometimes happen too: when there's a freak storm in June and the newly-shorn sheep die of exposure, we can be philosophical about it; when the weather turns suddenly ugly while the ram is with the ewes in the fall, we know we can expect fewer lambs to be conceived for the spring. But when a bunch of feeder lambs are in the barn two months after they should have gone to market, we look at them and blame ourselves for our bad management.

We have been well indoctrinated: we are responsible for everything that happens on the farm; if we fail it is our management that is at fault, always. This is surely the most insidious consequence of our industrial agriculture mentality: everything is supposed to be under our control. Only when it comes to the weather are we allowed to refuse responsibility. And even then there is the nagging doubt: could we not have arranged some shelter for the sheep? Could we not have forseen that storm?

There are certainly clear instances of mismanagement causing crop failure, especially for arable farmers: using the wrong chemicals or the wrong dosage, failing to harvest at the right time, seeding too late, planting too close. But on second thought, is the line so clear between mismanagement and crop failure? Are the grasshoppers an act of God, or a judgement on monoculture? Is it wise for us to provide such an attractive spread for insects that have their rightful place in a more diverse world? We are told that the spruce budworm is only destructive when faced with a forest of uniform age and species, again an invitation to a certain insect to "pig out" at our expense. Perhaps it is bad management to create conditions attractive to such "acts of God". When the rain failed last summer, it was reported that those farmers using the most chemical fertilizers were the hardest hit, because there was not enough moisture to make the fertilizer available to the plants; the organic farmers with healthier soil did not encounter such an extreme problem.

When the children used to complain and ask why they had to go out and do chores, we told them it was because we had a responsibility to the sheep. We had put them in a situation in which they could not fend for themselves, and so it was our duty to care for them. Our assumption was that we were in charge, in control. And when problems arose, we tore our hair and spent substantial amounts of time and money trying to correct our deficiencies as managers. It has been only recently that we have begun to wonder if some of our "failures" are not inherent in the system itself.

This fall, we found our feeder lambs losing weight instead of gaining. A number of them died; others eventually began to recover but were losing their wool. (When sheep are ill, particularly with a fever, the wool stops growing. When they recover and start growing wool again, there is a break in the fleece and often the old wool just falls off.) We took dead and dying lambs to the pathology lab, but they could find no common cause. What were we supposed to think? We finally narrowed the cause down to the barley we were feeding: it seemed to be the only variable. Of course, by the time we realized what was happening it was too late, we were on another batch of barley. We are told that the chemicals used here or there in feed production – herbicides, pesticides, fungicides – are all safe as rain, but was the barley toxic? Was the fault in our management?

It is precisely our high level of management skills which leads us to specialize, in this case to work with age- and breed-specific groups. Good management demands that as many of the sheep as possible lamb at the same time so that they can be handled as a group. Now we wonder if many of the disease problems are not directly related to having a large number of animals so similar in age and susceptibility together under such intensive management. The point is, this strategy of developing uniform groups of animals that can receive appropriate treatment *as a group* is essential if the two of us are to be capable of keeping enough sheep to earn anything approaching a living wage from them. It is, in fact, essential to good management under an industrial system of agriculture.

Must we, then, assume individual responsibility for these "crop failures"? Or are they an inherent part of that same skilled management which imposes such requirements on the wiles of nature? Would it be reasonable to suggest that crop failures, for the livestock farmer and for the arable farmer, are in part due to the fact that we are no longer one and the same?

Perhaps we should interpret crop failures in an entirely different manner: not as a failure to manage skillfully or diligently enough, not as our failure to have done enough research or applied enough technology, but as a judgement on our management system itself and, even more importantly, on the notion that we can or even should manage everything according to our very limited insights and understanding of the world we live in.

from *The Ram's Horn*, April 1985

SOME THOUGHTS WHILE FALL PLOWING
AL SLATER
St. Mary's, Ontario

October is the plowing month. It's a time when the tractor is on "automatic pilot" with its front wheel stuck in the furrow. Watching the rich black soil turning in three ribbons behind the plow promotes a lot of thinking.

The land I am plowing has been in hay or pasture for three years straight. This means that in the whole three years the land has not been plowed or re-seeded. It has not been bare at any time so no wind or water erosion has occurred. The land being turned over is full of roots and worms: a healthy state of affairs. We try to run a *low-entropy* farm. We are labour intensive. Our cows go to pasture in the summer and we feed them hay and grain in the winter. Most of our land is covered in grass and hay so we don't have erosion problems. With this kind of crop rotation we need no pesticides and not a great deal of fertilizer. Our energy requirements are low because our machinery is small and old to match the small amount of crop we grow each year.

I come to the end of the field just as the ring-billed gulls fly in to feast on the worms. They are beautiful birds, vibrant, raucous as they glide down with heads turning to search the ground for worms. But we cannot allow all our worms to be systematically eaten by these hordes. So I reach for the .22 sitting on the tractor. I take a couple of shots to scare the birds off. They all lift off then circle and land again. Sadly, I accept my next task. I draw bead on an unfortunate gull and pull the trigger. Thousands of gulls rise and leave for an hour or so. But one takes a couple of steps then flops on the ground. I run over to break its neck so it won't suffer. Its body lies there, a cool wind blowing its feathers, serving as a warning to gulls not to land. The body haunts me as I travel round and round the field. I hate shooting birds.

But why am I plowing during the day like this? Most years I simply plow at night when the gulls are not feeding. But this is the year that I have to accept the reality of the market. Consumers are using less beef and dairy products. Some, like ourselves, have cut back a little on meat for health reasons. Others, including some of our friends, are starting to see vegetarianism as some sort of moral statement. For us on this dairy farm it means that we have made a substantial cut in our cow herd. More land has to be plowed and planted to something vegetarians will buy and eat. They don't eat hay and pasture so our rotation won't be quite as good. There will be less roots and worms in our plowed ground in a few years. Our land won't get as much manure as it has in the past. If things get much worse we will be back to using chemical weed control because our choices of crop rotations to kill weeds will be severely limited.

I don't want to complain about soybean growers or people who use them. Soybeans are an important food crop. But the crop worries me. In Asia soybeans are grown using labour intensive methods. In the rest of the world soybeans have become a "high-tech" crop. In Third World countries like Brazil land has been taken from the peasants for multinational companies who grow soybeans for export while local populations remain malnourished. Here in Ontario land planted to soybeans remains bare in the spring until early June. Soil is subject to wind and water erosion for a long time. I suspect that a good deal of organic matter is oxidized by the sun during the long days at that time of year. Beans seem to like a fine seed bed and they grow close to the ground so the land has to be carefully levelled at planting time for proper harvesting. By the time the beans are planted the soil is worked so fine that very little structure remains. After harvest the land is black again because the bean straw provides very little coverage. Some bean stubble gets planted to winter wheat but the rest lays black and vulnerable all winter. I really hope I don't have to start growing soybeans.

As I start down another long furrow I am left with a lot of questions. Will my soil ever be as good again now I am forced to cut back on hay and pasture in the rotation? Will there ever be as many worms again? How much new machinery will be needed to match the increase in crop acreage? How will it be paid for? And how much more fuel will be used? Will people around the world be better fed as we switch from animal production to grain and soybean production? Is there not already a glut of beans and grain while people are starving?

I look up from the tractor wheel rolling down the furrow. There in the middle of the farm are the two oaks standing side by side. They first put their roots into the soil 130 years ago when my great-grandparents first came here. Over in the pasture are the cows. Their ancestry reaches back to that time on this farm too.

Some people are vegetarians who reject animal products. Some people are bankers who reject us as inefficient. Some people are polluters who send acid rain and fouled air over our land. Are these people rootless?

from *The Ram's Horn*, Dec. 1985

ON BEING A SOJOURNER
B.K.
Brookland, Pictou Co., Nova Scotia

A few evenings ago I went for a walk at dusk, checking the sheep and viewing the farm from the hill across the brook. I was moved to tears by the quiet, the beauty, and the pathos. The sheep, once I spoke, recognized me and paid no attention, except for those nearest who looked up. I realized that they had all been born and raised here; they know the farm better than I do, in a way.

The pathos accompanied the realization that even after 14 years here I know so little of this place, this land and its life. I am only a sojourner, a transient, here (like the sheep) only briefly; but unlike them, in that brief time I presume to take charge and to order this territory the way I want to. The old stone fences in the woods remind me of how rapidly the mark I have made can fade. I guess I've never really become a modern farmer: I've been a little too ambiguous to achieve that sense of certainty that seems to be essential to industrial, technological, capitalist production.

Sojourner is an interesting word: it means someone who is on the move, but who has stopped for a while. If farmers everywhere regarded themselves simply as sojourners, would we lose that sense of mastery and become more gentle and accommodating?

Yet there is a contradiction, for the farmer must also put down roots, be committed; it is as much a question of being owned by the land as of owning it. Does this mean staying put? Or might it mean being part of a community (it was once a family) that stays put for generations and puts down roots? What farming needs is a commitment to a place, without domination. Others will come after us, and what is left for them is up to us.

Sojourner is a Biblical word, and there is an analogy here with the Christian life, and the Biblical notion of the people of God. Sure, it is difficult to live with all the contradictions, but that is what faith is all about. Our culture runs into problems of stewardship – and good agriculture – when we want to eliminate risk, when we try with all our might to determine the consequences of all that we do by gaining (so we think) ever greater control over every step of the process. This is what leads us into our dependence on agrotoxins of all sorts, into our practices of monoculture, into our pursuit of uniformity, into factory farming.

Surely it is the delicate balance of the sojourner, between the need for roots and the need to move on, that is worth the seeking.

from *The Ram's Horn*, September 1985

CHAPTER 7

THE FAMILY FARM AND THE RURAL CRISIS

According to the 1986 census, Canada's population was 25,354,000, and only 4% of this total was "rural: farm" while 76% was urban (defined by Statistics Canada as communities of 1,000 or more with population density of 400/sq. km. or more). In 1956 the comparable figures were 67% urban and 16% rural: farm (the balance in both cases is described as "rural: non-farm").

While there were 293,000 "census farms" in 1986 (defined as "an agricultural holding with sales of agricultural products of $250 or more"), 260,745 of these had sales of $2500 or more.

As an Ontario dairy farmer put it, "Farming is probably much less a way of life today and more of a business operation than it was even 10 – 15 years ago, and although there is still that way of life tied to it, that's not the primary reason why people are there anymore."

When we hear the words "farm crisis", and read about record farm incomes in one column and farm debt in another, it is hard to make sense of it all. Many Canadians are fond of their rural roots and there is hardly an agricultural bureaucrat to be found who won't tell you how he comes from a farm, has a farm, or has visited farms as a child. There is a lot of sanctity surrounding "the family farm", but along with the new realism about the condition of marriage and the family, it might be well to work towards some realism concerning the family farm.

There are significant values and experiences that are implied in the concept of the family farm. The physical labour in which every member of the family took part is not an experience urban dwellers can easily imagine. The self-reliance of farm and community, living close to nature, the experience of the seasons and the power and wonder of life forces, whether expressed in the early spring racket of the peepers, the troublesome mounds of the ground hogs, the sprouts pushing their way above ground or the bleat of a lamb or the moan of a calf as it gets a hold on life, are all experiences beyond the urban realm. While reviewing family photographs of early days on the farm, we had to laugh when we realized that practically every picture of my daughter as a child had her holding a baby lamb, a chicken, a cat, or even the bull!

The imagery and the language always refers to *the* family farm, or simply to farmers, as if there was the generic farm or farmer, all virtually identical, like no-name peas and ice cream. But our experiences have not been uniform, nor have they been uniformly positive.

There is no single class of farmers any more than there is a standard farm family. Shared characteristics and problems and hopes, probably, but some farms are cold industrial businesses while others are "inefficient" human communities. Some farmers take pride in being businessmen while others are primarily concerned with their stewardship of the land and the life of their community. Some farmers have taken every opportunity to expand, buying out their neighbours along the way, while others have stubbornly refused to follow the urgings of the bankers to borrow and expand. Some farm children are taught to represent themselves as model suburban kids, while others are shunned by their classmates because their clothes are hand-me-downs and because they do chores before school every morning and after school every afternoon. These same kids may well enjoy at the same time the psychological health of knowing they do significant work, just as they can enjoy their physical strength and abilities. But who off the farm appreciates these increasingly devalued skills?

Industry does not hold people in high regard. Neither does capitalism. Since the 1960s the official vision of industrial agriculture has included as much capital and as few people as possible.

The 1969 Federal Task Force Report, *Canadian Agriculture in the 70s*, drew up a model for agriculture in 1990 and summed it up in these words:

> There will be a substantial reduction in the number of commercial farms. Some will be family farms but all will be rationally managed, profit oriented businesses. Farm mergers and consolidation will result in much larger units, not primarily for increased production efficiency, but to structure units that are large enough to afford better management.[39]

In the succeeding 20 years, the pressures seeking to define the farm and the farmer in this way have not relented. It is almost a wonder there are any other sorts left.

Late in 1988 the Farm Credit Corporation published the results of its 1988 farm survey. Among other things, it illustrated, with numbers, the process of polarization – what the agricultural economists call "rationalization" – among farmers. It did this by dividing all farms into one of three equal categories according to gross sales, total assets, and percent net worth.

The one-third of the farms with low sales had only 15.3% of the total assets, 7.8% of the total liabilities, and 4.1% of the total sales of all farms. Those with medium sales had 26.6% of the total assets, 23.2% of the total liabilities, and 18.3% of the total sales of Canadian farms. The one-third with the highest sales had 58% of the total assets, 69% of the total debts, and 77.6% of gross sales of all farms.[40]

The picture that these figures paint of the family farm are revealing indeed. The report comments: "It does not necessarily follow that the net farm income followed the same pattern as gross income." In other words, the farms with the biggest gross incomes owe the most money and are therefore paying a lot of interest. They may leave little or nothing for the family to live on. It is also probable that there is a direct correlation between the debt, the gross sales, and the industrial quality of the farming. In plainer words, the best farmers, in terms of stewardship and community, may be those with the least debt and the least sales. They may also be living as well as the high velocity farmers.

So it may be high time to take apart the notion of the family farm, like the ultra-filtration of milk which we discuss in Chapter

11, and separate it into its component parts to see what we are actually left with. Then we might want to make a social decision about what parts we want to keep and how we want to put them together.

The alternative is to observe what is happening and accept it as inevitable. If we do this, then we ought, at least, to be aware that there are others involved in this inevitability who are much less resigned or fatalistic.

There are two major elements of the farm crisis: first, the transformation and disappearance of the traditional family farm; and, second, the financial crisis facing a large number of farmers whose debt is greater than their equity and whose cash flow, like that of a Third World country, is not enough to cover the interest on the debt, much less reduce the loan outstanding.

The financial crisis in agriculture is not necessarily the same thing as the crisis of the family farm. Food production is now dominated by large commercial enterprises that may still be legally owned by a family, or a family-owned corporation, but they are already too large to conform to the traditional understanding of family farm. On these farms, the primary role of the family is that of enterprise manager rather than the principal supplier of labour, and its large amount of capital may be controlled, if not owned, by external lending agencies. So while these farms may be nominally owned by the families working them, the role of their creditors (which often includes chemical and fertilizer companies) in their management, like the role of the World Bank and the IMF in the management of Third World debtor countries, may be greater than most would like to admit.

By contrast, the traditional family farm is an enterprise in which virtually all of the labour is supplied by members of the extended family, in which management is not separated from the labour itself, in which responsibility for decision-making may be shared among those doing the work, and in which capital requirements are small enough for the family to actually own the equity. It may be a farm that has been built up over more than one generation, in which the grandparents continue to have a role. Such a farm can be passed from generation to generation without the burden of debt, the grandparents being cared for out of the continued operation of the farm, rather than being pensioned off and shipped out, requiring cash withdrawal that depletes the farm operating resources. Very often, in this picture, there have been hired hands, but they functioned both structurally and socially more as uncles or children than as hired labourers. (I recognize that this analysis leaves out the issue of authoritarianism and patriarchy.) With minimum cash flow and an extended family as the working unit, there was little opportunity for the wage differentials that alienate labour and management in industrial agriculture.

What has been valued in this model and is remembered is the integrity of the enterprise. Labour and management are not only non-adversarial, they are united in the same persons. Nor is capital treated as a separate aspect: it consists of the land which the family is working, which is not regarded as a marketable commodity; the limited machinery, which is basic and durable, again not to be bought and sold, but bought and repaired and used more or less forever; and livestock and stored feed or grain. Cash flow, which has become *the* criterion of capitalist enterprise, is marginal, though this is not to say that it is inessential. Within a form of self-reliant agricultural production, *minimal* cash flow is a sign of health, whereas in industrial agriculture the health of the enterprise is judged, by the banks, by how *big* the cash flow is. Thus news reports talk about gross farm income, which reveals absolutely nothing about the actual health of the farm or agriculture in general. As a largely self-sufficient sheep farm, we had a rather low gross income, yet we knew that our net income, what we had to actually live on, was often greater than that of the hog farmer with ten times the gross income. The hog farm bought much of its feed and carried a large debt, we did not.

Another way of distinguishing the traditional family farm from the modern industrial enterprise is in terms of the primacy of labour rather than the primacy of capital. If most of our agricultural production is now carried on in highly capitalized industrial enterprises employing wage labour under family management, then what are we talking about when we say we want to save the family farm?

The largest number of farm units are still more or less traditional family farms, but they have always counted on off-farm employment, such as teaching, nursing, driving the school bus, fishing, or working in the woods for cash income. Mythology notwithstanding, the North American family farm has hardly ever been a viable enterprise in the sense of providing an adequate or complete income for the whole of the small community that lived on it. So it should not surprise us that today commodity prices, outside of supply-managed dairy, eggs, and poultry, do not return enough to keep the family or the farm going. As the need for off-farm employment increases, the family farm disappears.

The question must be asked again: What is in crisis, and what do we want to save?

There is a financial crisis facing small family farms simply as a result of commodity prices being below anybody's costs of production. That is, however, very different from the debt crisis facing large, capital intensive industrial operations that expanded on a speculative market and are now caught short.

The heart of the crisis, in fact, may not be farming as a way of life, but the ownership of the means of production: of machinery and land and buildings (the visible signs of status and success). There is, after all, a substantial difference between farming as a vocation or a way of life, and farming as the ownership and management of capital. There is no inherent reason why a farmer must own the land he or she works. What is important is security of tenure.

The cause of much of the farm crisis is the debt which was incurred when money was loaned and land purchased on the basis of the inflated and speculative land prices of the late 70s and early 80s. Like the fishing boats left high and dry in the Bay of Fundy at low tide, as land prices declined (about 50% since then) the farmers who bought at high tide are left stranded. In part it is the farmers' insistence that they have to own the land they farm which is now eliminating the farmers. (We return to this issue in Chapter 15.)

While farms may still be growing in acreage and capital, or debt, farms as social units have been shrinking for years, accompanied by a decline in the rural community.

THE CRISIS IN RURAL COMMUNITY

Rural Manitoba: we drove into the yard just in time to join a neighbourhood barbecue. It's not much of a farm community anymore since most of the neighbours work in town at one job or another. Not long ago 300 people or so lived there. The big grain elevator on the main line was at the centre of the town. The talk that evening was of how the elevator was going to be closed down. "Rationalization they call it." Then the focus of the conversation shifted to the "new" 3-bedroom house that had been built for the elevator manager not many years ago. The people we were visiting had moved three vacant houses already from the "town" onto a single property so that they could enjoy some sort of community life. One of the men present was an assessor in a nearby town, and he said, "You wouldn't want to pay more than $8000 for the house alone. You would have to spend that much on a new foundation and then pay moving costs, and in town (25 km away) they can't give houses like that away for $25,000."

So what is to become of rural Canada?

If there is a crisis in agriculture, increasingly it is being overshadowed by the crisis of rural community, or, more precisely, the destruction of rural community. What is mourned as farmers depart the land, as the government and its Market Economy agents dismantle the infrastructure of rail lines and schools and public services, is the possibility of community. *Rural Dignity* sprang up in 1986 in one of Canada's remote corners when the Conservative government announced the rationalization of rural post offices, by which they meant another step in the dismantling of the infrastructure of rural society. Rural Dignity was a good name for a movement that understood that self-respect and identity are essential to any community. Take away the post office, the grain elevator, the feed mill, the bank, the farm machinery dealer – a town cannot survive with only the coffee shop to hold it together.

When we moved to the farm in 1971 we had a ring-down battery-powered telephone. The phone came with the farm and made us members of the Saltsprings Mutual Telephone Company. The switchboard was tended by Mrs. Roblee who was 82 when she retired. That was when we had to admit defeat and join Ma Bell. The first fall we were there, though, the line needed repair. Old Herbie had cut some trees off his farm for poles, and we hired a backhoe to dig the holes. It took about eight of us all of a Saturday to replace the poles that had rotted off and to put up the wires that had been laying on the ground, in some places for quite some time. But I met the neighbours as I would never have otherwise. The meetings of the phone company took place in Donald's kitchen, or in Isabel's – with "lunch" afterward. Progress came to Saltsprings, and that same year we moved to Saltsprings the local school was closed. (The original district school half a mile up the road had been closed years earlier.) Our kids spent two hours a day – from age five – on Isabel's bus to get to a school that effectively took away another one of the reasons for there being a community in Saltsprings. Later the post office was moved down the road so it could be right on the highway, but not many could walk to it then. Progress and rationalization were not good for that community.

Who wants to live in near-total isolation without neighbours? The kids finish school, having clocked one lifetime already in school-bus confinement, and move on. There is no longer a community for them, so what happens to the farm becomes more a matter of nostalgia than choice. The crisis is social, but it is the result of the reduction of a society to nothing but a Market Economy.

Who will mend the social fabric when everyone is busy making money?

CHAPTER 8

ELECTRONIC FOOD

IT ONLY COUNTS IF IT MOVES – TECHNOLOGY AND CONTROL

As you go through the check-out counter of a large supermarket the clerk passes each item over a scanner. In 1985, 692 stores in Canada had scanners. By 1988 the number had risen to 950, and these 950 accounted for one-third of the total grocery store sales of $36-billion. Only unpackaged items like carrots, and some unmannerly and awkward packages like bottled water, have to be manually punched in. (The carrots themselves will probably soon be genetically engineered so that each one contains its own barcode.) The scanner, and the barcode on the label, are virtually our only reminder of the fact that the computer both controls and makes possible the food system we take for granted.

The scanner, of course, is connected to an electronic cash register with a printer that can give you an itemized slip – or with an artificial voice that can tell you what you have purchased at what price! But this register is just the visible tip of the iceberg. The information entered into the computer at that terminal is not just the price of what you have purchased. It is a precise list of everything that you have purchased, and this happens with each customer. In other words, every item that goes out of the store (paid for, that is) is immediately recorded as a debit to inventory in the main computer. Since everything coming into the store is likewise entered, the manager knows precisely, at all times, what is on hand. He (or she) knows what is moving and how fast (referred to in one trade magazine as "warehouse velocity"). The manager can also monitor the productivity of the clerks.

Employees can now use cards that look like credit cards to check in and out. They can do one or more jobs a day at different rates of pay and, with the card, are paid for the work they do. If more hours are worked at a particular section than scheduled, the computer can tell who worked those extra hours and when. All the retailer has to do is find out why.[41]

Soon you may even be scanning your own groceries, if the clerks get pushy and demand living wages, and you will then pay a cashier who is really more of a bank teller. This will probably require, in turn, a magnetic security tab on each item, like the higher priced clothing in Zellers. This is, of course, a somewhat fanciful scenario, but the system is moving rapidly in that direction.

From electronic space management to custom-generated coupons at the cash, computer technology is providing radical and required changes in the way retailers do business.[42]

While this process may simply seem to be efficient, without electronic information processing to keep track of the 7000, or 15,000, items stocked at any one time this huge and highly centralized system would simply not be possible.

Inventory control – knowing how much of what is where – is only the beginning. The computer can also tell the manager what is moving and what is not. Timely specials and discounts can keep the sluggards moving before they really back up and foul the system. (This has its good side in helping to reduce spoilage and waste.) If the retail outlet is owned/managed by the wholesaler/supplier, then the process can go back a step to include the warehouse. So the warehouse and the store are integrated, though spacially separated. Some independents try to overcome this disadvantage by turning their stores into warehouses. Thus the "warehouse store" with its goods stacked in cartons overhead or underfoot.

Still another integrating step can be taken. If the wholesaler is large enough, it can extend its control backwards to the processor. Again, information is the key. The processor may now be owned by the wholesaler or may be operating under contract. Either way, the processor becomes simply one sector of transformation as the product moves continuously from the farm through the system and out the retail end. The processor/distributor can often pass this control on further back and specify to the grower or farmer what is to be provided, of what quality, and when, as we saw in Chapter 4. This results in contract farming where the buyer/processor may well specify the seed to be planted, the date it is to be planted, which herbicides, pesticides and fertilizers are to be used and when, and when and how the crop is to be harvested, often after some chemical has been applied to assure that the entire crop is ready for harvesting simultaneously on the day the harvester has been booked.

McCain's, based in New Brunswick, is a good example of the intimate relationship that can develop between processor and farmer. McCain's has chosen to work the area that includes farm input supplier, farmer, and processor, replicating its way of doing business in country after country. It controls the potato system from its position as major world processor, with operations in eight countries and global sales of more than $2-billion, leaving the retailing to others. (One of McCain's 1988 expansions, in France, requires an additional 4500 hectares of potatoes to be produced. In all likelihood, these, too, will be Russet Burbanks, as we saw in Chapter 5.)

Facilitation of this integration and centralization by means of electronic information processing – the computer – has not been confined to the PDR (processing-distribution-retailing) sector. The farmer, or farm corporation, may well be using a computer not only to keep financial and farm records, but to make day to day management decisions using computer software that is also designed to assist the farmer in utilizing all the latest advances in technology, like the transponder hanging on the cow's neck that is her personal key to an electronically controlled feeder which meters out feed according to her current milk production. If it is good management to gear up the cow in this way, it is certainly considered sound financial management to gear the farm into the commodities market, utilizing the computer again, to speculate on the futures market, politely called "hedging", with the farm's potential grain crop in order to stabilize returns and increase profits.

> New approaches to business and technology would help pig produc-
> ers. Certainly, keen financial management and intensive computeri-
> zation will be basic to the surviving enterprise, along with extensive
> use of futures and hedging to "soften the downside". [43]

But all computer software expresses an ideology; an organizing principle or logic. The designers (programmers) of agricultural
software will express the ideology of their employers, and if they
work for the agricultural establishment, whether government or
corporate, their programs will more than likely express the Market ideology of productivity, efficiency, and competitiveness, as
well as the private ownership of the means of production!

The majority of farmers are no more likely to be able to design
their own programs than they are likely to have the capacity to
design and build specialized equipment for field work, though they
may know very well what they need. So the technology comes to
define the choices.

Soon after we started farming, I realized that I had two
choices when faced with the tremendous number of stones in the
fields. I could either try to pick them all off, or I could smash them
back down into the ground. The latter seemed the more practical
course, and through a British immigrant farmer I succeeded in
importing a heavy "Cambridge" ridged-ring roller from Britain designed to do just that job. I never saw another such roller, though
many farmers admired mine. The technology that was commercially available was rock picking machines. These are big and expensive and generally operated by contractors, but they are used
because it is the technology that is available, even though a very
small tractor could utilize my simple roller at much lower cost.
This illustrates what I would call technological determinism. [44]

The seed the farmer plants may itself be the product of similar information processing. Working with the seed company, probably owned by one of the chemical companies supplying the additives required in the production process, the processor may be
telling the university researcher (funded by the corporation) what
characteristics are desirable.[45] The researcher will then engineer
the seed to meet those specifications using the same information

processing technology to model the alternatives before actually creating them. This is the way in which Rapeseed was transformed into Canola. As in the supermarket warehouse, electronic information processing provides the means to identify and select from the multitude of characteristics and combinations.

> All that is needed to artfully explore the inordinate number of possible product combinations in the genetic, chemical, and microbial realms of agriculture is a computer.[46]
>
> ---
>
> NutraSweet is looking at the next generation of high potency sweeteners and we're using computer modelling to do it. We know the size and shape of molecules common to sweetness and once we've isolated them in sweet-tasting products, we try to build molecules that resemble them.[47]

The seed finally winds up being merely an *envelope* for the package of genetic information created or assembled by the genetic engineer. Thus control over the production process passes back to the designer of the seed itself, and the requirements and characteristics of the seed and what it produces will have been determined according to a particular economic ideology. The farmer and the processor may think they exercise some control over what they can do, but their freedom is severely limited by what has been designed for them. This is another example of technological determinism: technology being developed and used by one interest or corporation to determine what others can and should do.

Yet we tend to regard technology as harmless or neutral. This book is being "written" on a computer, so I am engaged in electronic information processing both externally and internally. Internally my brain and central nervous system are processing information via electrical impulses while externally the computer is doing the same thing, as an extension of my self since it is inert unless activated by me. In this sense it is just another piece of technology making human work easier, more fun, more demanding, or whatever. The technology does invite collaborative work, information sharing, and perfection in writing.

But the technology I am utilizing has its own logic and the program I am utilizing is the product of a particular culture. The computer I have chosen to use operates on a zero-based (digital) system, and what I can do with it is limited by *its* logic; in other words, I have chosen to accept its limitations on my logic, even while I develop a critique of this logic. I have to operate within the limits as well as the logic of the technology I have chosen.

The diminishing gap between technology and its products, between the living and the inanimate, is aptly illustrated by the story of a "virus" discovered in the fall of 1988 in a computer network in the U.S.A. *Science* magazine reported that, "The main computer network for researchers in the U.S. and overseas was disrupted for two days last week as managers tried to kill an electronic virus injected by a graduate student. . . . The 60,000-machine system, some experts insist, was not infested by a true virus but by a relatively benign "worm". Unlike a virus, which breeds by insinuating its own logic into existing programs and making them bear its offspring, a worm remains self-contained. It lives off weaknesses in the host's logic. This particular worm did nothing but reproduce madly."[48]

This computer *virus* was not like a cancer virus that devours its host, though it could have been designed to do that. It was, however, self-replicating and had it gone unnoticed for a longer period might have done untold good in dismantling the military apparatus. Infecting the medical records of a large hospital, on the other hand, could be disastrous. There is an eerie similarity between the salmonella bacteria crippling the British poultry business and the computer virus. So integrated are both systems that to get rid of the diseases it is almost necessary to shut the entire systems down.

Access to and control over information may sound harmless, but what information you are provided with or have access to determines the context of your decisions. Equally, lack of information means lack of decisions and leads to passivity and powerlessness.

The seed – the carrier of genetic information as well as the means of production – refers not only to what we normally think of as those things we plant in the ground in the spring, but it also refers to the sperm, the ova, or the embryo. The term "designer genes" is catchy, but it is also accurate. If the issue of control is significant, then we must look carefully at who the designers are and who they work for, just as we must in considering computer software design. In turn, we should consider whether we have any control over those corporate designers, and what social and moral criteria guide them in their decision-making.

The farmer who is not happy about accepting these corporate designs will soon find him or herself in a position very similar to that of the small genuinely independent retail grocer. Both count on a local or specialized market and are essentially operating speculatively. They have virtually no control over their selling prices. To the extent that they are labour intensive, they are unattractive targets of corporate takeover. It is precisely for these reasons that the dominant corporations increasingly encourage the independent operator, both as farmer and as retailer. These so-called independents create an impression of alternatives in the system, of variety, and of opportunity for individual entrepreneurs. In addition, they provide a degree of service that no electronically controlled business dependent on turn-over and discounting can provide. (An industry survey of franchisors indicated that quality was their number one strategic goal as well as their number one "success factor".) The superstores will even pursue this logic to the extent of having independent operators within the super-stores themselves, dealing in fresh fish or bulk foods, flowers or a deli. These low-volume specialty shops or kiosks can increase the attractiveness of the entire store and increase the patronage, thus adding to, rather than subtracting from, the high-volume sales of the main store.

In the same way, there is a new interest in agricultural smallholders who will produce quality food, such as organic or "natural" beef or vegetables, and specialized products such as goat cheese or wild-flower honey, products that the electronically controlled corporate or giant family farms cannot provide. (Provincial and Federal assistance programs have taken this into account in recent years.) Nevertheless, when bulk food marketing was re-introduced a few years ago in health food stores, it was not long before the major chains followed suit. In the same way, the "natural" or "organic" categories are quickly captured by the capitalist marketing system and then side-lined to the position of a high-profit niche product.

My son brings home a bag of chips and we try them out: they are Hostess (owned by General Foods which is owned by Philip Morris – don't be fooled by the Canadian flag on the bag!) Gibney's, "Crispy Slow Cooked Homestyle Chips" tasting very much like the local, "handmade" chips – Miss Vickie's, Millie's, and others – that hit the market as specialty products a few years ago as people began to seek healthier and more tasty food. (In chapters 14 and 15 we look more closely at organic and sustainable agriculture.)

Agriculture has reached what [has been] called "the second industrial divide." . . . At such a point, a mass production technology can undergo a fundamental change and become a "craft" system. Some features of craft technology are the ability to respond to changing demand rapidly, a high degree of regional coordination, and an increased dependence on information systems. . . . Low-input farming is another craft system. It can flexibly and rapidly respond to changing market conditions, and it emphasizes regional production, processing, and sales. It also requires more information.[49]

The monolithic supermarkets of the 60s lost their public appeal rather quickly, as, for the urbanite, industrial agriculture lacks the charm of the family farm in the same way. In the sophisticated marketing of the food system of the 80s, it is imperative to develop the appearance of diversity and intimacy. The technology of electronic information processing has not only facilitated the centralization of the distribution system but also its apparent diversification and variety. Micro-biology and genetic engineering would not be what they are without the computer, and neither would the Weston/Loblaws empire.

FAST TURNS AND CONTINUOUS FLOW

Pity the poor tomato: designed in a university lab and propagated in a corporate lab by means of tissue culture before being set out in a greenhouse. It grows some, and then is transplanted. It grows some more and bears fruit. No time to stand still. The fruit is harvested, roughly, but it hardly notices because it has a tough skin. Maybe being designed is better than just being bred. Then the tomato is packed and transported, like a charter vacation flight, and then pushed around a warehouse, transported some more, stacked and fondled and dumped in a cart just to be picked out again and weighed and rolled down a chute into yet another wagon, transported yet again and, mercifully, consumed shortly thereafter. Rather dizzying, all that constant movement. Hardly time to get your breath, much less to ripen.

Central to the logic of the food system controlled through electronic information processing is constant movement. The measure of productivity in this system is like water through a turbine, or the electricity meter in your home: it is the flow that counts. You are billed for electricity in terms of the flow of power. Volts is a measure of potential, amps is a measure of flow, and watts (volts x amps) is the measure of volume. You are charged for the number of watts consumed. Quantity is a function of movement.

> The profit margin on confectionery runs from 25% to 35% as compared to the 15-17% margins realized on heavily featured items in the grocery aisles. However, retailers and suppliers have to remember that on items that generally sell for less than $1, fast turns are important.[50]

But technology makes its demands. To be manageable electronically, the goods must be uniform, from seed or fetus to apple or cereal box. Every kiwifruit must be the same size in order to fit properly into the container that will be handled by electronically guided equipment into and out of the warehouse. The potatoes must all be close to the same size so they can be sliced according to an electronic formula for processing into chips in the most effective manner – after they have been mechanically harvested and graded and washed. Watch the cars going through an automatic car wash some time. It is movement that counts. The car is attached to an endless moving chain to go through the car wash. The potato or the milk or the chicken is little different. Processing tomatoes are literally floated out of the special steel trailers that haul them from the field onto the conveyor line for processing.

They disappear into a building and the cans emerge at the far end already packed in cartons for shipping, with the labels of half a dozen different companies on them. The local farmers were forced to adopt the new technology – the trailer-mounted steel tanks – if they wanted to continue to grow and sell processing tomatoes. No more utility wagons hauling hay in June and baskets full of tomatoes in August.

The consumer, too, must perform its function in this process. Its function is to consume. Advertising, packaging, and all the rest of marketing will provide all the help they can, but the product must *move* and if the customer will not buy it, the product must move anyway: to another store, to the sanitary landfill, to the food bank. That is why the big chains support the food banks which provide a socially acceptable dump or "outlet" for the products that are not moving and defray, through tax write-offs, the costs of those that have to be dumped. As we saw in Chapter 1, since the recession of the early '80s food banks have become sophisticated and integrated elements of the food system. Those who have been marginalized by being deprived of buying power are reintegrated by those willing to be surrogate customers on their behalf. Sales, cash flow, and the very health of the economy demand it.

The consumer responsibility to the food system is to consume, to keep the product moving. This enables the stores to keep fresh product on the shelves, keep the stock clerks working on a uniform schedule, keep the stock moving through the warehouse – in one side and out the other – keep the processing plant operating every day with a minimum of labour because it can be automated if uniform. The system will *source* its supplies wherever it can, regardless of politics or geography. Price, reliability and consistency are the only concerns. The raw materials will be processed wherever it suits the buyer, in most cases. That, in turn, will largely depend on labour conditions, and hence, politics, but wherever, it will all be made possible by modern communications technology.

> Retail managers are encouraged to use software like *Spaceman* and *The Third Generation* to help them utilize their computers. *Spaceman* "ties floor planning, fixture engineering, market research, data processing, buying, merchandising and other related departments into a common merchandising operating environment. . . . Technology has altered the methods used to market and merchandise the front end (by the cash register) and it can help increase the profitability of an already profitable area."[51]

"Spaceman" is not a bad description for the scenario being played out at the other end of the food system as well, as the introduction of HYVs (High Yielding Varieties) changes the relation of labour and the biological production process and moves agriculture, too, in the direction of a continuous process operation.[52]

CHAPTER 9

FOOD AS INFORMATION

OWNING THE MEANS OF PRODUCTION

While it may seem far-fetched, there is no significant breach between the control of inventory in a modern food warehouse by means of electronic information processing, the direct debiting of your account at the check-out counter of the supermarket through the same electronic information system, and the electronic manipulation and modeling of genetic information. Your groceries can be kept track of by means of electronic information, and so can the human genome (the complete genetic coding).

Electronic information processing has transformed the food system before our very eyes, from the scanner at the check-out counter to the university laboratory designing new saline-resistant wheat or producing synthetic porcine growth hormone. But the computer has become more than simply a means of managing and controlling information, and even more than the means of creating and controlling vast systems. It has actually become the *means of production*, and this raises the question of ownership and what are called *intellectual property rights*.

Accumulation of capital – the theoretical essence of capitalism – is only possible on the basis of private property, that is, the legal ability to exclude others from access to certain property which is the means of production. Thus Brazilian peasants are cleared like the trees off the land to make way for corporate soybean production, or landless peasants in the Philippines starve because they have neither employment on nor access to the land of the idle sugar estates, idle because of the lack of export markets for sugar. The reason why there has not been significant land reform in countries like the Philippines is obvious: there is a profound contradiction between uncontrolled ownership of land and universal access to land as a means to production and survival.

While there has, for some time, been a legal recognition of ideas as property, reflected in patent and copyright law, we are now reaching the final stage of the sanctification of private property. We no longer speak of ideas. Now it is *intellectual property* and its protection (privatization) by means of *intellectual property rights*, is extended to any novel or particular configuration of information that anyone wants to bother with.

The logic of private ownership reveals its ultimate conclusion, and perhaps its absurdity, when the information over which exclusive ownership is being claimed is itself the means of production and of its own reproduction.

Information is no longer understood to be simply a passive phenomenon *about* something. It is now understood as an active phenomenon *for* something. The productive potential of information is most dramatically revealed by the fact that it is the genetic information coded in the DNA that produces (or determines) a particular protein. Thus information comes to be understood as a means of production, and the owners of capital insist that it must be privatized. This is the fundamental issue behind *plant breeders' rights* and corporate ownership of seeds.

Genetic information, the genetic coding in the chromosome that determines the life form, is regarded in the same way that a new herbicide or a new form of packaging might be. According to the theory of intellectual property rights, the researcher/inventor who comes up with a saline-resistant wheat, or rather the corporation or university that employs him or her, should be able to patent and claim as its private property the genetic information that distinguishes, *and produces*, that wheat. By the same logic, the biologist who develops a cow that is resistant or immune to mastitis should be able to patent that distinctive genetic coding. From this reductionist perspective, there is very little difference between a computer program and a set of chromosomes. Both are simply a collection of certain bits of information in a specific relationship to each other.

It is then but a short step to the patenting – claiming the property rights – of a modified human embryo, one that has been subject to gene therapy on the basis of need established as a result of amniocentesis on the embryo *in utero*. In other words, once the principle of intellectual property rights is accepted, there is no natural or inherent limit to the claims that can be made. Human characteristics could be patented and licensed for production just the way a McDonald's hamburger or a new lettuce plant could be. Do you prefer curly leaves (hair) or straight, long stems (legs) or short?

Proctor and Gamble Company officials attributed the decision to cut back on cookie production to alleged infringements by three companies on patents for soft-texture Duncan Hines cookies.[56]

The long-term implications of the legal recognition of the private ownership of genetic information, the means of production and reproduction, must be considered now that the U.S. patent office has granted patents on microorganisms (the U.S. was the first country to allow a patent, in 1980, on living matter, a microorganism that liked to eat oil spills) and also granted Harvard University a patent on a living mouse early in 1988. Actually Harvard did not get a patent on the mouse itself, but on the genetic material it contained: a gene that made the mouse highly susceptible to human cancers, specifically breast cancer, so that it could be used more easily in cancer research. The real significance of this for the food system is that Harvard, or the corporation to which it licensed the production rights, Monsanto, can collect royalties on the progeny of that original mouse for 17 years! All one needs to do is apply that to the hog or poultry industry to realize the potential.

The extent to which the argument for privatization can be taken is fully articulated in a study published in the United States. Addressing the question of "What biotechnological subject matter, if any, is excluded in principle from patent protection?" the authors argue that, "The basic tenet of patent law is that subject matter is in the public domain only if it is *both* old (lacks novelty) *and* obvious (lacks inventive step)". On this basis they then claim that, "*Only if it is in the public domain* should it remain free for all to use."[54]

The patentability requirements of novelty and inventive step are sufficient to preclude the patenting of any products which are already reasonably available to man [sic]. . . the public remains free to do anything that it could have done prior to the inventor's discovery of the so-called "product of nature". In other words, the *actual* "product of nature" can never be patented and does remain free for all. . .

And what of the philosophical tenet that all products of nature must remain "free for all to enjoy?" . . . As noble as this precept may sound, it is of no practical utility for promoting progress in the useful arts. . . . "Products of nature" which are unknown to mankind are no more useful than are inventions that have not yet been made.[55]

Having virtually equated "man-made" with any- and everything that is discovered, the authors then advise that other countries should adopt "the U.S. concept that everything under the sun that is man-made should in principle be able to enjoy the innovation-encouraging reward of patent protection."[56]

In other words, everything in the world – Creation itself – is private property waiting to be discovered, to be owned. There is nothing in the public domain until it is discovered or invented and made public through the patenting process because the public cannot enjoy what it does not know about, what has not been discovered. The Creator God, then, will have to argue the case in patent court.

To illustrate some of the difficulties and issues raised by the pursuit of ownership rights: Genentech, Inc., got U.S. federal approval for its synthetic human growth hormone Protropin in 1985. At the same time it got it protected as an "orphan drug" giving it seven-year commercial protection. It is a recombinant DNA product with a 192 amino acid sequence. Later Genentech developed another human growth hormone with a 191 amino acid sequence and applied for approval, and protection. However, Eli Lilly and Co. has also developed a human growth hormone with the same 191 amino acid sequence but via a different process. They, too, want approval and protection, claiming a significant difference because of the different process. Under patent law as it stands, a process can be patented as well as the product if it is novel and distinct.

AGRICULTURAL TRADE AND INTELLECTUAL PROPERTY

The December, 1988, meeting of the General Agreement on Tariffs and Trade (GATT) in Montreal was an important event because, for the first time, agricultural trade was on the GATT agenda. Officially the major issues were liberalization of agricultural trade, the elimination of non-tariff barriers, the harmonization of health, safety, and packaging regulations, and intellectual property rights. At the top of the practical agenda, however, was the purported agricultural subsidy and trade war between the United States and the European Commission (EC) acting for the European Economic Community (EEC). In spite of its own massive subsidization of agricultural commodities export through its Export Enhancement Program, the U.S.A. insisted that all responsibility for the disastrously low global grain prices lay with the agricultural export subsidies of the EC. The ideological position of the U.S. was that all "trade distorting measures", including subsidies of every sort, should be removed by the year 2000.

At the end of the week, nothing had been settled and intellectual property rights were hardly even mentioned because the United States adhered to its long-held position that it, and it alone, would define both the agenda and how the issues were to be resolved.

Of the 96 or so countries participating in the GATT, 70 are what are loosely termed "developing". The people of these countries have interests, by and large, very different than those of the wealthy North. However, the question of *whose* interests were actually represented at that meeting and others like it applies to every delegation. Perhaps it was a senior executive of the Australian multinational, Elders, that was really the voice coming from the Australian chair, or perhaps Argentina was advised by the Vice President of Bunge and Born, one of the five biggest global grain traders. And it may well have been a senior Vice President of Cargill who sat behind the U.S. table, along with the man from Dow Chemical. Certainly the voices heard were not those of urban slum dwellers, landless peasants, or native communities. The voices we heard spoke for transnational corporations (TNCs), the banking fraternity, and the Market Economy.

Brazil, for example, is one of the *Cairns Group* of 13 grain-exporting countries, along with Canada, Argentina, Chile, Colombia, Australia, Hungary, Indonesia, Malaysia, New Zealand, the Philippines, Thailand and Uruguay. It is difficult to understand what the people of these countries have in common that their governments can pretend to speak with one voice. The trade representatives of the Brazilian Government do not represent the two-thirds of their own people who are hungry and without sufficient income to buy food because the resources of the country are being devoted to the development of export agriculture, hydro-electric projects in Amazonia, and payment of the $6.7-billion interest (1988, est.) on their massive debt of $120-billion to the banks of Canada, the U.S., and elsewhere.

Or take the example of Sri Lanka: 200 years ago, Sri Lanka was self-sufficient in food. Along came the British Empire which imposed an international division of labour: Sri Lanka would produce tea for the global market, rather than rice and textiles for itself. (The British were protecting their own textile industry, even though they had to import the cotton for it.) After the British came the Green Revolution which brought HYVs (high yielding varieties) of rice and another form of dependency; and then came the U.S. with its wheat which altered their rice-based culture. Now Sri Lanka is being told to grow things like oil palms for the global market, yet another division of labour.

Who, then, did the representatives at the GATT meetings speak for, and who were Canada's delegates and what interests did they represent? Did the Canadian representative, John Crosbie, speak for the farmer members of the three Prairie Wheat Pools, or for the international grain traders with offices in Winnipeg and Toronto? Did he represent the dairy farmers with supply management, the rural communities of Canada, or the elite of The World Bank? The easiest way to answer the question is to look at who benefits from low grain prices, from chemical monoculture, from the public subsidies that are passed through the farmers to the banks and the seed and chemical companies, i.e., who benefits from the policies of the Government and its corporate advisors.

For example, from 1984 to 1987, under an "executive exchange" program, David Gilmore, a Vice President of Cargill Ltd.

(the Canadian subsidiary of Cargill, Inc.), was on loan from Cargill to Agriculture Canada to assist in drafting agricultural policy for the Conservative government. Cargill continued to pay his salary while he occupied an office on the top floor of the Carling Building beside the Deputy Minister of Agriculture. Similar things have occurred in the U.S., and probably elsewhere, for many years.

The press reports from the Montreal GATT meetings gave voice to those demanding the right to pursue corporate profits or a reduced deficit through the sale and export of agricultural surpluses, not those who demand fair trade and a chance to feed their own people. The press did not discuss the profound differences between *trade* in agricultural goods and *export* agriculture.

Trade implies on-going relationships with trading *partners*, and to be on-going the terms of trade have to be sustainable. Sustainability requires fairness and justice between sectors in the food system as well as sustainability in supply, i.e., production.

Export, on the other hand, is essentially opportunistic, a one-way transaction that seeks to maximize returns, whether to "service" foreign debt or, as in the case of the U.S., to pay for domestic and global militarization. As Canada, the U.S., the EC and others push them, agricultural exports have little or nothing to do with reciprocity or fairness. *Comparative advantage* is precisely *not* based on sustainability or justice. The pursuit of advantage is the pursuit of power.

The Canadian government's major concern at GATT appeared to be the protection of our *right* to export surplus grain, in spite of the fact that it is export agriculture that causes starvation and death for millions of people by denying them the opportunity to produce food for themselves. The dependency on agricultural production for export also leads to the destruction of rural Canada. Canada's position is rationalized on the grounds that its economy as a nation-state has always depended on the export of agricultural production, particularly grains. [57]

However, all the discussion about trade and export subsidies could soon be overshadowed by the further development and recognition of intellectual property rights. The future of agriculture around the world will be shaped by how the issues of patenting and biotechnology are handled. The trade/export issues will be insignificant if the germplasm of every food crop and farm animal is patented by one or another of a handful of TNCs who are also the producers of agricultural chemicals: Ciba Geigy, Bayer, and Sandoz (Swiss), Rhone Poulenc (French), Cyanamid and DuPont (U.S.A.), BASF (German), and ICI (British).[58] Those few people or businesses actually growing the food will be reduced to the status of franchisees, dependent for all their inputs on a few corporations and liable for royalties to the same corporations on everything they produce. The state will perform its assigned role of patent police and collection agent.

The U.S.A. wants common international standards on patents, trademarks, etc., and a general agreement on how to enforce the rules. The Chairman of Dow Chemical, an advisor to the U.S. delegation, was reported to have said that the U.S. will take matters into its own hands if it doesn't see progress. "In our discussions with India and Brazil, we will just have to make them understand how strongly we feel about the matter."

Given the role of transnational corporations in our present food system, if the U.S. were to win its way and impose on every other country its definition of intellectual property and insist that the member states enforce the rights granted to the corporate sector, then the integration of the food system, from the seed to the fruit on the table, would be virtually complete. Discussions about agricultural trade would then focus on the mechanisms of royalty payments for patented swine and corn, or on inter-corporate competition in Third World markets.

With the extension of intellectual property rights, Ciba-Geigy could develop a high-yielding variety of bean resistant to their herbicides and pesticides available in the Third World and then coerce governments into protecting their own monopoly position. Third World farmers would find themselves little more than either corporate labourers or contract (franchise) farmers purchasing their inputs from a single TNC supplier which would dictate the terms of trade for the crop on the global market. In Thailand today, farmers are not permitted to grow the native varieties of rice. The government requires them to grow only the hybrid varieties, the seed for which the farmers have to buy for each crop.

CHAPTER 10

FEEDING THE FAMILY: CONTRADICTIONS OF CAPITALISM

THE HUMAN BEING VERSUS THE MARKET ECONOMY

While the current political climate encourages us to think of an economy mainly in terms of production and accumulation, an economy is more correctly defined in terms of the distribution of the resources of a household or community, whether that distribution is equitable or not. Who qualifies as a member of the household is basic to the definition of any economy.[59]

THE INVISIBLE HAND

We justifiably take pride in the achievements of Western Civilization, or what we like to call Democracy, and the Enlightenment, by which we mean Reason and Science. The economy that has emerged from this very particular historical context, using the tools of technology and industrialization, appears to have produced impressive abundance and wealth. Unfortunately, the benefits of this economy have not been made universally available. On the contrary, they have been only very unevenly distributed within the northern democratic states and not at all to the vast majority of people of the world, who, it now begins to appear, are increasingly deprived of even elementary participation in the benefits of an economy. (The net transfer of wealth from the poor and indebted countries of the Third World to the wealthy of the North is now well documented. The Caribbean and Latin America transferred something like $28.9-billion to the industrialized world in 1988, $12-billion more than in 1987. The IMF and World Bank are the primary agencies of this transfer, but the commercial banks also play their part. This does not include net transfers of wealth out of the Third World by corporations, which are almost impossible to document since much of the transfer occurs *within* the corporations.)

The wealth produced, or accumulated, by the industrial capitalist economy is often regarded, at least by conservatives, as justification of its morality. That is, it must be good to have produced so much. On the other hand, rationalism would claim that it must be scientific to have worked so well.

The explanation offered for the inequities resulting from this economy is that those designated as losers have not followed the rules or played the game properly: they have arbitrarily or irrationally intervened in the scientific and rational processes and distorted their economies. The explanations given for intervention (that it is motivated by concerns for justice, equity, conservation, or ecology) are dismissed, by and large, as irrational. Nevertheless, the ecological consequences of the industrial development policy as advocated by agencies such as the World Bank, on behalf of multinational corporations, are now being challenged, and some would claim modified, by pressure coming from efforts like that of The World Commission on Environment and Development[60] and the environmental movement.

If the purpose of an economy is to organize the resources of a society so that the basic needs of everyone are met, then what has gone wrong that the number of hungry and malnourished is growing? Has it been the failure or the consequence of the theory of capitalism itself?

The foundations were being laid in philosophy and science for the Industrial Revolution and the rise of rationalism and reductionism two hundred years ago. Adam Smith, currently the patron saint of neo-conservative economists and free market capitalists, wrote *The Wealth of Nations* in 1776. His notion of "the invisible hand", which is the magic that is supposed to guide the Market

Economy to function in the best interests of everyone, was first expressed in this context:

> [Every individual generally] neither intends to promote the public interest, nor knows how much he is promoting it . . . he is in this case, as in many cases, led by an invisible hand to promote an end which was no part of his intention. Nor is it always the worse for society that it was no part of it. By pursuing his own interest he frequently promotes that of society more effectually than when he really intends to promote it.[61]

Smith had no illusions about either the social relations that would result, or the moral character of those who were the leading merchant capitalists and practitioners of his philosophy of his own day:

> Wherever there is great property, there is great inequality. For one very rich man, there must be at least five hundred poor, and the affluence of the few supposes the indigence of the many. [62]

> Civil government, so far as it is instituted for the security of property, is in reality instituted for the defence of the rich against the poor, or of those who have some property against those who have none at all.[63]

It is a cultural and political disgrace that the "science" of economics has come now to so dominate our public life that the primary purpose of the economy and the state has been allowed to become the organizing of markets for privately tendered goods, services, and capital, that is, the organizing of an economy for the purposes of personal gain rather than for the just ordering of the household and the feeding of the entire family.

The acceptance of *the marketplace* as the functional organizing principle of a society is remarkable in that it has worked so badly and the cost has been so high. The affluent lifestyle of the average North American, the achievements of science and technology, the glories of military might, and the phenomenal overproduction of food, have all been premised on the deprivation of the majority of the human population and the exploitation of natural resources. The historic epoch of rationalist industrialism has been brief, and the wonders of the market economy have been shared amongst only a few of the globe's people. As the UNICEF report, *Status of the World's Children 1989*, puts it, "policies which lead to rising malnutrition, declining health services, and falling school

enrollment rates are inhuman, unnecessary, and ultimately inefficient."

> Among the public in the industrialized world, it is still widely
> believed that money is flowing from rich nations to poor nations
> to assist in the struggle against poverty. Ten years ago that was
> true . . . *Today that flow has been reversed.* Taking everything
> into account – loans, aid, repayments of interest and capital –
> the southern world is now transferring at least $20-billion a year
> to the northern hemisphere.[64]

> For almost nine hundred million people, approximately one
> sixth of mankind, the march of progress has now become a re-
> treat . . . . After decades of steady economic advance, large areas
> of the world are sliding backwards into poverty.[65]

If we attribute to economics the status of science, and if we
regard the production of surplus food as a sign of the effectiveness
of science and technology, then we will probably also accept the
deprivation of others as the price of progress. If our fate is indeed
guided by Adam Smith's "invisible hand", then our ethical and
moral concerns can be laid to rest as sentimental intrusions.

Smith, however, did not believe that self-interest necessarily
coincided with the common good. "Profit hunger conflicts with
public interest" in that it always aims at a monopoly, which he
defined as "infamous covetousness . . . which does not shrink from
terrorization and crime." The corrective, in Smith's view, was
competition, but he could hardly have been expected to foresee
the consequences of his theory: the ineffectiveness of competition
in controlling monopoly, the extent to which the pursuit of self-interest has not fostered the common good, the inability of the Market Economy to organize and conserve resources for sustainability,
and, most fundamentally, the exclusiveness of the household
served.

One of Smith's contemporaries, Jeremy Bentham, recognized
the consequences of the practices which Smith advocated, and, in
the words of Karl Polanyi, offered this solution to the problem in
an argument reminiscent of current rhetoric about social welfare
programs:

> Labour should be dealt with as that which it is, a commodity
> which must find its price in the market. The laws of commerce
> were the laws of nature and consequently the laws of God. Ben-
> tham believed that poverty was part of plenty. "On the highest

stage of social prosperity," he said, "the great mass of citizens will probably possess few other resources than their daily labour, and consequently will always be near to indigence [poverty]."[66]

WORKERS AND CONSUMERS

Among the many contradictions of capitalism is this: on the one hand there is the persistent drive to find or develop new markets both for the products of industry and for the capital expropriated from the economy. On the other hand, there is the equally persistent drive to maximize profit by reducing costs, namely the costs of raw materials and labour. As a result, an *antagonistic contradiction* arises: the market consists of customers, that is, people with money to spend, while at the same time labour is paid as little as possible.

The very system that devotes energy and resources to developing markets (major Canadian corporations spend a minimum total of $235-million per year on print and broadcast media food advertising alone), at the same time reduces large numbers of the global population to a level of poverty that excludes them from the system as customers. Henry Ford knew he had to pay his workers enough to turn them into customers for his cars, and John D. Rockefeller, whose philanthropy is largely responsible for financing the research that led to the Green Revolution, knew that capitalism needed both markets and a stable, welcoming political environment. Having accumulated a vast fortune by the turn of the century, Rockefeller created the charitable trusts whose good works he hoped would neutralize the all too evident inequities of capitalism and repel the threat of socialism as an alternative.

It was this same philosophy which led the Rockefeller Foundation to establish a research centre (CIMMYT) in Mexico for work in improving wheat and maize (corn). This centre, and a few others, became world famous as the pioneers and propagators of the Green Revolution which was based on the high-yielding hybrid seeds developed by these research centres. As Edward Yoxen points out:

[A] plausible and significant reason [for the Rockefeller Foundation establishing this work] is that American foreign policy-makers in the 1940s perceived Mexico as a strategically important country . . . that needed to be modernized without a revolution and linked harmoniously to the expanding U.S. postwar economy. The official version is that the Rockefeller Foundation was persuaded . . . to do something about world hunger. . . . As the program at CIMMYT developed it . . . represented "managed" social reform through strategic technical change, the hallmark of Rockefeller philanthropy. With a more "efficient" agricultural base would come political stability and an increase in international trade, particularly, as it turned out, for the products like fertilizers, pesticides, irrigation pumps, farm machinery and fuel required to make the new agriculture work and the new plants realise their potential yields. The Rockefeller initiative was followed by other foundations such as the Ford Foundation, which helped establish an International Rice Research Institute . . . (in the Philippines).[67]

COMPETITION

The ruling axiom of Market Economy theory is that our economic ills – including hunger and malnutrition in the Third World – can only be overcome through increased efficiency and productivity; by becoming more competitive. Yet the biggest "investments" being made in the food system are not in new or more efficient production facilities, but in take-overs and leveraged buy-outs of food processing and distributing companies. A leveraged buy-out takes place when a company is bought on the strength of its own assets rather than with outside capital. To achieve this, a company borrows a massive amount of money, often from a consortium of banks, for a very short term in order to gain the leverage to buy out another company. It then uses the assets of the company it buys to pay off the short term loans used to gain the leverage, either by selling off parts of the company or borrowing long-term against the value of its new assets. Thus businesses may change hands for billions of dollars with absolutely no investment in productivity or efficiency being made. The purpose is not to fulfil the public ideological goals of the Market Economy, but to provide a quick profit (instant gratification) for the owners, advisors and bankers.

Until late in 1988, the biggest leveraged take-over in history was that of Beatrice Foods by Kohlberg, Kravis, Roberts, a private New York company, for $6.2-billion, in the summer of 1986. Shortly afterwards, the same private firm bought Safeway (U.S.A. and Canada) for $4.2-billion. Then these records were broken in the fall of 1988 with the purchase of Kraft by Philip Morris for $13.1-billion, creating the world's biggest consumer products company. In the same vein, Nestlé bought Carnation for $3-billion in 1985, Weston bought Cadbury, and the list goes on. Finally, in December, 1988, Kohlberg, Kravis, Roberts succeeded in buying RJR-Nabisco for $25-billion! The four investment banks working for KKR stood to get at least $400-million in fees out of the deal.

Adam Smith would surely have difficulty reconciling this immense concentration of unproductive economic power with his theory about the need for competition if the pursuit of self-interest was to actually work for the common good:

> To widen the market and narrow the competition is always the interest of the dealers. . . . The proposal of any new law or regulation of commerce which comes from this order, ought always to be listened to with great precaution, and ought never to be adopted, till after having been long and carefully examined, not only with the most scrupulous, but with the most suspicious attention. It comes from an order of men, whose interest is never exactly the same with that of the public, who have generally an interest to deceive and even to oppress the public, and who accordingly have, upon many occasions, both deceived and oppressed it.[68]

An overview of our global food system reveals such immense contradictions and irrationalities that one might well wonder how the system continues to function. That it does is probably testimony not to its inner logic or the science of market economics, but to the immense resources and forgiveness of the Earth, whose stability and ability to absorb punishment is great enough that until recently we have been able to ignore the global consequences of our activities.

POPULATION

The Market Economy is based on the economics of scarcity, or more precisely, the idea of scarce resources. Nature is held responsible for inequities because she is stingy and does not provide enough to go around. The other way of stating this same approach is that there are too many people. If a society does not want to address the issue of distributive or social justice – making sure that every member of the household is fed – then a theory of scarce resources and overpopulation can serve a useful function in maintaining class inequities: there simply isn't enough to go around.

The result is that there are many people who believe that unless we continue to become more productive, we will face disaster within a few decades as the growth of global population outstrips the growth in the food supply. This argument has been put forward by the same class of people since the days of The Rev. Thomas Malthus 200 years ago. Their argument has been consistent: poor people tend to multiply at a higher rate than rich people, and left unchecked *they* will multiply beyond the ability of the earth to provide for them. Thus the poor are themselves believed to be the cause of their own poverty. Malthus recognized that those who could afford to have many children refused to do so, but he never drew any conclusions from this observation. Two hundred years later it is still those who hold the wealth and power, and those who identify with them, no matter how poor they are, who seem to be the ones most worried about the deprived of the world multiplying. One can hardly help but conclude that their arguments and advice, and even policies, are more protectionist than charitable.

However, human reproduction rates are, not surprisingly, closely correlated with economic well-being: the harder the circumstances, the more children a family will have in order to have more breadwinners and to ensure that there will be enough that survive to care for the elderly. The easier the circumstances, the smaller the families, and until a woman can be sure that all her children will survive, it does not make economic sense to her to limit her family. As a study done for the Brundtland Commission expressed it, "The problem is not one of global food production being outstripped by population. . . . The problem has three aspects: where the food is being produced, by whom, and who can command it."[69]

The constantly shifting definition of *family*, in practice if not in public ideology or theory, is a healthy reminder of the danger of limiting our notion of family. A healthy economy, with a healthy community, will care for everyone within its physical domain with a reasonable degree of equity. (The Mosaic Law called, as did Jesus in turn, for including the widow, the orphan, the alien and sojourner.) One could describe this as enlightened self-interest, as who knows when *we* might find ourselves on the outside, but self-interest of a very different sort than that encouraged by capitalism and the Market Economy.

CHAPTER 11

FROM COW
TO COMPONENT

THE EFFICIENT COW

Efficient, productive, and *competitive* are the three magic words of the Market Economy. They are being used to facilitate the reduction of agriculture to a lifeless industrial process under the control of a limited number of transnational corporations. Dairying is a good example.

The Canadian Holstein *is* efficient and productive. The dairy industry is also highly organized and very efficient, largely due to the leading role played by provincial milk marketing boards and commissions (which are *not* profit-oriented businesses) and by supply management. (Supply management is the practice of actually tailoring supply to demand by having an agency, such as a milk marketing board, license farmers to produce milk and to control supply through quotas. The Market Economy exercises no such rationality.)

Socially, the Holstein cow is probably a little more competitive than a Jersey or a Hereford cow, although Holstein psychology has not yet given firm indications of how inherently competitive they are. In terms of productivity, the tremendous increases that have been achieved with Holstein cows as producers of skim milk are impressive, but these gains are also probably the greatest threat to the Holstein's true competitiveness. To become *competitive* in the industrial-economic sense, the Holstein has been forced to become so dependent on the farmer, his machinery, and his purchased protein concentrates, if not feed, that she would quickly turn into a wreck if left to fend for herself in the way most beef cattle rightly are.

The dairy industry is among the most high-tech sectors of the food system: technological intervention affects the breeding of the cow, her feeding, her milking, and finally the processing of her milk.

For the sake of genetic improvement and gains in productivity, not even breeding is simply breeding anymore. It is a contrived process of selection and manipulation that could conceivably see a cow give birth to a calf that was put together in a lab out of patented genetic material from a dead bull and a dead cow. The aim would be to gain productivity and efficiency. As it is now, dairy cows are seldom bred directly by a bull, which is, instead, usually kept at a special facility where his semen can be collected by technological means, frozen, and then transported and inserted into a particular cow for a fee. Due to this very effective distancing, the cow may never see a bull in her entire life. She will live in a unisexual world alongside other black and white production machines.

The feed (forage crops and grain) for this production machine may itself have been genetically engineered, not to be more nutritious, necessarily, but to be more resistant to leaf miner or a nematode, or to a particular herbicide or insecticide. This engineered feed can be augmented – or perhaps this would be better stated as, the cow's metabolic processes can be enhanced – by various manufactured substances such as hormones and antibiotics, again in the name of productivity and efficiency. If the cow manages to be long-lived in spite of all this, she will be fortunate indeed, because the average number of lactations for a Holstein is about $3\frac{1}{2}$, meaning that she is four years old when sold for hamburger. Given that old-fashioned cows could easily milk for 8 to 12 years, modern production practices do not appear to be very efficient, although it is claimed that the price for four-year-old Holsteins as cow-beef does make this financially attractive when balanced against the cost of replacement heifers and the returns on milk. But being financially attractive in a certain situation does not necessarily make the practice efficient.

What becomes of the milk that results from this process depends on a lot of factors having little to do with human nutrition and much more to do with the market, shelf-life, and corporate profit. It is worked-over in a variety of ways before it is finally consumed, some of it as whole milk, much of it as a constituent of some food product, as we have seen.

If our Holstein cow is thus being continuously improved, the question that must be asked is, what is the net gain to society, if any, resulting from this supposed gain in efficiency?

As the word is used today, efficiency refers to the ratio between inputs and outputs. To make any sense, of course, the inputs and outputs have to be carefully described as to character, amounts, and cost, as in a recipe. In a capitalist culture, efficiency is usually evaluated in terms of short-term *numerical* efficiency, that is, reducing the numbers and/or costs of inputs in proportion to the numbers and/or costs of the outputs. This numerical efficiency deals only with the current use and configuration of the parts, not with the functioning of the whole, either on its own or in relation to others, or over the long term.

Even within the context of short-term numerical efficiency, being more efficient can, in part, be attributed to the practice of shifting certain costs, such as that of home milk delivery, from the accounting of the seller to that of the buyer (from the processor to the consumer). The milk still has to get from the store or dairy to the home, and there is a cost to someone in that effort. The externalizing of certain costs is not the same thing as actually becoming more efficient, that is, getting the milk from the cow to the consumer with the least gross expenditure of energy, according to the thermodynamic law of efficiency (see Chapter 14).

Once the cost of getting the milk to the consumer has been taken off the books of the dairy and shifted onto the consumer, who still has to take the time to get the milk (among other things) from the store, the consumer must be convinced that the lower price, or the convenience of being able to take the time to get milk whenever it suits, is a real gain. But the consumer is still paying for the delivery. There is in this, also, the assumption that there is a person at home available to take the time to pick up the milk: in the current reality this actually becomes yet another stress on the typical single, often female, head of the household and/or wage-earner. Socially and humanly, this may actually be seriously inefficient.

At the other end, as the number of dairy farms and dairy processors has decreased, the distances the milk has had to be hauled has increased. This process of reducing the number of farms and the number of dairies is referred to as "rationalization" and it has been done in the name of efficiency. As a result, milk hauling may cost the dairies and the farmers less, but that will be in part because the cost of the highways over which the milk is hauled, including snowplowing, is paid for by the public.

The corporation, the enterprise, or the individual that is most successful in externalizing their costs is likely to be the winner in the Market Economy. They will probably also be the recipient of public subsidies of one form or another in spite of their vociferous pieties for the Free Market.

For example: Winnipeg-based Cargill Ltd., one of Cargill's 800 subsidiaries in 55 countries, did not let principle stand in the way of a $4.5-million grant from the Government of Alberta towards the costs of its new beef packing plant at High River. There is nothing special about Cargill; this is common practice. (Cargill Inc. of Minneapolis is the world's largest grain trader, with 25% of the global trade, as well as the largest exporter of both Canadian and U.S. grain and the third largest meat packer in the U.S.)

Within this logic, "competitive" describes the character of social relations between individuals seeking what is best for themselves. Those that are successful, the winners, are by definition "efficient". If, as a result, some people get rich and others starve, that is an unfortunate consequence of an efficient market economy, not a moral issue. So even though the living standard of hundreds of millions of people is lower now than it was 15 years ago, the World Bank assured the public at the end of 1988 that "numerous Third World countries registered the benefits of the tough economic reform programs they instituted in earlier years."[70] These "benefits" were not described, nor was the fact that these "reform programs" were instituted at the insistence of the World Bank itself and are among the causes of growing poverty.

The social ideology of bourgeois society is that the individual is ontologically prior to the social. Individuals are seen as freely moving social atoms, each with his or her own intrinsic properties, creating social interactions as they collide in space. Society as a phenomenon is the outcome of the individual activities of individual human beings.[71]

The pervasiveness of this logic is reflected in the following comment by the President of the dairy processors' lobby:

We should take a new look at milk, and use technology in our industry the way it is frequently used in other industries, that is, instead of saying milk is the end, say milk is the beginning. What is milk? Milk is simply the agglomeration of constituents. Let's break it down and recombine it in as many ways as we can.[72]

The premise of a Market Economy that the individual pursuit of personal gain will result in the greatest good for the greatest number is a matter of faith, and it only makes sense in the context of the reductionist logic that the whole is nothing more than the sum of its parts. As soon as we raise our sights, however, we can see that this individualism is anything but efficient, and is, in fact, leading to global ecological disaster.

MARKETING TECHNOLOGICAL WONDERS

Trade shows can be fun. They are intended to sell new technology, new equipment, and new services, and to provide a meeting place. They can also provide a wonderful display of the character of an industry and where it is going. The "Food and Dairy Expo" held in Chicago in 1987 presented the stainless steel splendour of the dairy processing industry in all its apparent complexity and diversity, or at least the diversity of ice cream novelties that satisfied my need for lunch for two days.

Fancy ice cream is a big money-spinner, so there were flavours and fruits, ice milks and non-dairy ices, yogourts and rich ice creams, along with the very expensive gleaming technology required to mix, sterilize, pack and freeze the fluids and forms. It was also intriguing to see how many different countries were represented by equipment manufacturers and ingredient suppliers.

Among the manufacturers of dairy processing, packaging, and handling equipment, ingredient suppliers (nuts, frozen fruits,

flavours, extenders, emulsifiers, etc.) and related corporate interests present at the show, was Cargill. Cargill was present under
two flags: as a manufacturer of a new Maltose corn-based sweetener and as recent purchaser of a Dutch chocolate company. The
Dutchman at a chocolate display explained that he understood
that Cargill bought his company because Cargill is after 25% of
every food commodity on the world market.

That did not explain Cargill's involvement with Maltose,
which, as they advertise it, is a new generation of corn sweeteners,
produced by enzyme technology and significantly sweeter than
High Fructose Corn Syrup (HFCS), which has already wreaked
havoc with Third World sugar cane growers. In the "free market"
of the United States, sugar from domestic beets or imported cane
costs food processors about 30 cents a pound while corn sweeteners are marketed by Cargill, among others, at 2 or 3 cents less.
Interestingly enough, this is because the sugar industry in the
U.S. has had enough political strength over the years to maintain
a protected market at a price above the real cost of production.
Supplementary imported sugar receives a higher than world market price but is imported on a quota basis. These quotas have been
severely reduced in recent years, reflecting the inroads made by
HFCS in the sugar market, primarily in soft drink production.

Cargill is not the only peddler of sweeteners, among which
NutraSweet is probably the most high-profile. Actually NutraSweet is the trade name for aspartame made under patent protection in the U.S.A. by G. D. Searle. (Searle is owned by Monsanto, one of the chemical giants that has moved heavily into
biotechnology and other "value-added" lines.) In the U.S. market
Searle is enjoying a seven-year lease-on-life granted to NutraSweet by the U.S. Government through the extension of its
patent – fortunately denied in Canada.

The expiration of patent protection in Canada did not, however, open the market to NutraSweet's competitors as one might
expect. Apparently the majors (companies such as Coca-cola, General Foods, etc.) were offered one-year contracts for supply by NutraSweet at prices so attractive that generic aspartame was virtually shut out of the market. (The contract price may have been as
much as 50% below the price charged before the patent expired.)

This one-year hold on the market gave NutraSweet time to try to consolidate its public appeal through a massive advertising blitz in 1988.

In its promotional material NutraSweet is described as "the only sweetener made from protein components . . . . It is made of two protein components (amino acids) . . . found naturally in a variety of foods." Does that make it a natural product? The manufacturers do not claim that it is, but it raises the interesting question about what is "natural" at a time when new processes are being discovered almost daily to engineer new products out of naturally occurring substances.

Another wonder is Solka-Floc, described in company promotion as, "a family of finely divided fibrous products manufactured from purified cellulose . . . the ideal ingredient for the food industry because it has no flavour or odour, is essentially non-caloric, and contains at least 99% dietary fibre." The sales rep did not hesitate to explain that the product probably came from Canadian maple, beech, or birch. At home we call it wood pulp. Its advantage over bran is that it does not tie up (or "bind") essential minerals as it passes though the digestive tract. How natural can you get!

Then there was BiPRO, described in a company brochure as, "the first of a new generation of dairy ingredients that combine enhanced functionality, full solubility, and neutral flavor. BiPRO is a wholly natural ingredient produced from pasteurized whey through selective ion exchange. The unique ion-exchange process selects out the main functional proteins . . . for concentration and spray-drying. . . . Good taste, good nutrition, increased profits; they're all yours with BiPRO enriched beverage products."

TECHNOLOGICAL PROCESSES

Some of the most intriguing new technology is for filtration, with new developments of old technology now able to purify even the most noxious waste. These filtration processes are made possible by the ability to produce polymer and ceramic filters that can filter out, or allow to pass through the filter in a continuous process, molecules of specified weights or sizes. Thus there is low-pressure ultra-filtration, high-pressure reverse osmosis, and gas perme-ation under vacuum. Not only is this technology capable of dis-charging water that is probably cleaner than the city water that went into the system, it can also separate food into even more dis-criminate components than other methods developed thus far.

Some of the applications of ultra-filtration, which is a rela-tively low-energy technology, are in milk concentration (water re-moval) for cheese making, concentration of whey, clarification and concentration of fruit juices, water purification, and concentration of maple sap.

The potential implications of this technology are a challenge to the imagination. Like virtually all new food-processing technol-ogy, it is designed as a continuous-flow process. CIP (Clean In Place) is a good example: dairy equipment, from pipeline milkers to pasteurizing and packaging machinery, are cleaned without dis-assembly by washing cleaning agents through the continuous sys-tem.

One exhibitor explained that his company had tried to install ultrafiltration on a California dairy farm of 2,000 cows or so, but apparently that did not work out well due to the very high level of technical skill required to operate the equipment. The aim, of course, is to reduce the costs of transporting all the water in whole milk (thus facilitating the distancing of the cows even further from the consumers). The most successful applications of the process so far have been to concentrate whey and turn what has been a pol-luting, unusable waste into usable components and clean water.

The reduction of a whole product, such as milk, into its com-ponents (fats, non-fat solids, water, etc.) by a relatively inexpen-sive process is very appealing, and it is consistent with the trend in the food system to gain as much flexibility as possible for those in control. Breaking the raw materials down into essential compo-nents for subsequent recombination into as many different prod-ucts as possible, in turn facilitates centralization of processing, dis-tribution, and corporate control. Food production begins to take on the characteristics of "world-class" automobile production: a handful of corporations source their components around the world and ship them by the container-load to the final market region for final assembly into several different models.

The potential reduction of whole milk into fractions, or components, parallels the reduction of corn into components engineered for certain purposes, such as the maltose described above. Add other developments in food science, like the discovery of new enzymes and new uses for them, and it appears likely that the market engineers may soon be the only ones deciding the forms of food that we will eat. Under the regime of corporate food, the goal will continue to be profit maximization, not nutrition.

> Industrial research and development is revealing the molecular composition of food in all its aspects, from its behaviour in industrial processing to the biochemical determinants of flavour . . . . Due to fractionation and industrial reconstitution, [the food] system has become much more complex with more intermediate processing steps separating field and table. Thus the final food product may be at several removes from its original rural form.[73]

> These advanced techniques threaten to *trivialize* agriculture, transforming it into one among several competing sources of organic matter for biomass conversion and fractionation.[74]

Accompanying these developments in production technology are new food preservation and packaging techniques. Food packaging has had a preservative function for ages: storing in brine, canning, even burying in the ground. But the precise tailoring of food design, processing, and packaging is now reaching levels of sophistication that would have been unimaginable even one generation ago. A major breakthrough came in the early 1950s from the Swedish company Tetra Pak with the idea of aseptic (anti-septic, or sterile) carton packaging, but this technology has only really hit its stride in the 1980s. Aseptic packaging is a process whereby a food, in liquid form (so far mostly juices and dairy products), is put into a sterile package in a chamber of sterile (filtered) air. Hydrogen peroxide is the sterilizing agent because it breaks down as water and is absorbed as soon as it has done its job.

Combined with Ultra High Temperature pasteurization ("UHT" in Canada, "Ultra Pasteurization" in the U.S.) of the milk or juice, which virtually sterilizes the product, aseptic packaging provides extremely long shelf life. (Refrigerated shelf life can be increased from 16-18 days to 30-45 days.) While the elimination of preservatives is a plus, the minus is the package itself, a laminate containing inseparable, and hence unrecyclable, metal, plastic, and paper film. ("True to Nature – keeping food in good shape" is the heading of a Tetra-Pak ad.)

What all this does for distancing, centralization, and concentration in the food industry should be obvious, but what effect this sterilization of food has on nutrition is less obvious. So far, sterility seems to be regarded as an unmitigated good in the food processing industry. Cleanliness must be next to godliness and a long shelf life.

A U.S. dairy industry executive described his vision: "The future may even see hospital operating-room-type conditions in the handling of milk from farmer to consumer. I call this managing the environment."

On the other hand, there are some thoughtful people who contend that even traditional pasteurization destroys some of the more subtle nutritional qualities of milk, and as our analytical techniques become increasingly refined, we may discover that there is indeed some material basis for their position.

What we may discover, long after considerable cumulative damage has been done, is that the more we isolate, by sterilization, what goes into our bodily material composition, the weaker and more dependent we become as a living organism, very much like what happens to highly bred dairy cows or hybrid corn. We really know very little about the subtle and complex relations both among the various functions of our bodies and between these functions and our environment. Every step we take to "clean up our act" may, in fact, be deleterious in ways we cannot begin to describe but should be able to imagine.

BIOTECHNOLOGY

Biotechnology, as interpreted in capitalist business culture, is an interventionist program to gain greater control over the productive process. It deals primarily in the genetic information that controls both process and product which, in effect, become a means of production. That is, genetic engineering is an extension of the drive of rationalist and capitalist culture to gain ever greater control over the means of production in the pursuit of profit.

If we return to the Holstein model discussed earlier, we can see clearly that genetic information is crucial in every step of the process. Certain genetic information is selected, by a variety of processes, in order to produce a cow with specific characteristics. The alfalfa or corn she feeds on has also been genetically selected or engineered in order to produce a crop with specific characteristics. The resulting corn or alfalfa then itself becomes the means of producing the milk in the cow.

Once the cow has been milked, the milk itself becomes the object of other processes of biotechnology, such as breaking the milk down into its constituent components so that it can be engineered into some new food. This process of breaking down and recombination is itself a matter of manipulating genetic material (information), which continues to be a factor in the means of production.

The important issues in biotechnology are ownership and control, just as they are in every other field. But in biotechnology we have a peculiar opportunity to gain a new and profound insight into the paradigms of economic and political organization.

To oversimplify, the farmer may think that he or she is in charge of the farm. The farmer is certainly encouraged to believe this by the Ag Reps, bankers, economists, and others. But if we stop to reconsider our Holstein cow, the fact may be that it is the gene designers who have control. The farmer is increasingly bound to play a pre-defined role within the productive process genetically engineered into the cow, the feed, etc. As Robert Doyle puts it, "farmers are becoming tenders of genes they do not control."[75]

The farmer turns out to be only a *rentier*: the real means of production are the genes, chromosomes, and germplasm which are rented out to the farmer in the form of various genetic packages, like seed, cow, and herbicide. Were efficiency, and not control, the real interest of the owners of the means of production, then the genetic design and engineering department would pursue different goals. Doyle describes the emerging situation as "a coupling of genetic power with corporate power."

Agricultural research in both Canada and the United States has been almost entirely carried out in public institutions, universities or government research agencies, with public money. Yet today there is very strong pressure from the neo-conservative government-corporate alliance to privatize all of the publicly funded benefits. The agenda appears to be to have the public continue to pay for the basic research that is not commercially attractive while the private sector commercializes and reaps the rewards of whatever fruits the research bears.

One of the best ways to capitalize on publicly funded research is by obtaining patents and licenses on the commercial or potentially commercial results. And as we discussed in Chapter 9, when what is being patented is genetic information which is now available as a means of production, the logic of the private ownership of the means of production is complete.

Why is there no great public debate about this seizing of public resources through the application of Intellectual Property Rights?

> The first line of defense of the status quo is always ideology; if people believe that the existing social order, whatever its inequalities, is inevitable and right, they will not question it. In this way, ideologies become a material force.[76]

Modern science and capitalism both depend on the passivity of the majority of the population: profits are reduced to the extent that there is resistance to exploitation, whether in the simple form of a strike (where not instigated by the company for its own purposes) or in the more crude form of labour unrest that requires the discipline of state intervention, or, as in many countries, more harsh measures by private assassins or para-military death squads. Starvation is not regarded as sufficient reason for peasants to seize land or organize for collective bargaining.

However, it is much cleaner and more efficient if we all accept Science and Technology (the two words always appear together like Siamese twins) as the evolving self-determining phenomena to which we must adapt and over which we have, and can have, no control. Thus the propagation of technological determinism as a tool of the controlling interests. (In the next chapter we will examine the origins of this.)

There is another rationale for the increasing role of genetic engineering in agriculture and food production: biotechnology is touted as a way to reduce agricultural input costs and reduce the role of agricultural chemicals. This is attractive at a time when increasing food production *per se* is no longer the primary concern of most agricultural economists or food policy bureaucrats. The new official position is: produce the same amount of food more efficiently. (If efficiency equals output over input, then efficiency can be increased by holding output steady while decreasing input costs.) This doctrinal revision allows the agricultural economists to maintain their authoritative positions without an admission of failure or a loss of power.

Biotechnology is the new way for the primary producer to avoid the traditional trap of trying to produce more in the vain hope of getting ahead, an effort which, in a saturated market, simply leads to a lower price. Producing the same amount, or less, but at lower costs, should increase net returns. This is the promise of biotechnology, but it is just what has been promised to farmers for generations by those who control the terms of trade. Any increases in genuine efficiency by the primary producer are quickly taxed away by those who have effective control over the inputs and the market. In addition, any momentary advantage gained by one producer through the adoption of new technology is soon eliminated as other producers adopt the same technology. What this turns into is an endless quest for advantage through new technology. The real beneficiaries continue to be the manufacturers and salesmen of the technology and information.

If greater efficiency – producing at lower real costs – is really the goal, then one would seek to actually eliminate a cost, like the herbicide, rather than making the production process dependent on the increasing costs of sophisticated technology. Rather than locating or developing plant varieties that are resistant to disease or pests, the chemical companies are developing varieties that can tolerate the herbicides or pesticides that they make. Thus Monsanto is developing new plant varieties that are resistant to its glyphosate herbicide in order to expand the market for the herbicide.

CHAPTER 12

SCIENCE TAKES CONTROL

SIMPLIFICATION

The proponents of high-tech chemical-industrial agriculture frequently deride their critics by pointing out that we cannot go back to the good old days, etc. The inference is that we have become much too sophisticated, and life much too complex, to *go back*. The fact is, however, that simplification and oversimplification are among the major characteristics of our present high-tech computerized and capitalized food system. Farming was much more complex and diverse just 40 years ago than mainstream agriculture is today, and traditional polyculture which once supported whole populations where now we find starvation, was infinitely more complex than the simplistic solutions of plantation agriculture, the Green Revolution, and biotechnology.

> The practice of growing many crops, and even many varieties of the same crop, within the same field ensures against famine. The chances of several different crops and varieties all being destroyed simultaneously by the same pest or change in climate is remote. This is the agriculture of security rather than commerce.[77]

Superficially, our technological culture appears increasingly complex. One manifestation of this is the growing number of synthesized chemicals used in agricultural production: at the end of

1988 there were 4,000 registered commercial and restricted pesticides on the market in Canada. "Pesticides" includes herbicides, fungicides, insecticides, plant growth regulators, and anti-microbial agents such as wood preservatives and disinfectants. These 4,000 products are made from 466 active ingredients. If domestic (household) products are included, the figures would be 6,000 and 500 respectively.[78]

We have already described a very similar apparent complexity or diversity at the other end of the food system in the grocery store. This apparent diversity is also reflected in the complexity of farm machinery or of various diets. The impression is certainly not one of simplification, yet the major cultural aspect of modern industrial agriculture is monoculture, the growing of a single variety of a single species continuously on a vast scale accompanied by the elimination of every *competitor*, plant or animal. Compare this to a polyculture where every bit of solar energy, water, earth and space are utilized in the form of an intricate web.

Or compare the traditional varieties of dairy and beef cattle (Brown Swiss, Guernsey, Jersey, Shorthorn, Angus, etc.) that could once be found on Canadian farms to the monoculture found today with the Canadian Holstein, the Hereford, Charolais and a few other "exotics"; or look at poultry: there are only 22 major breeding companies in the world. In Canada, Shaver Poultry Breeding Farms Ltd. supplies the birds that lay about 40% of all the eggs consumed in Canada. Their goal of supplying 30% of the layers in all 90 countries in which they sell has already been achieved with white eggs. Approximately one egg in three around the world is derived from Shaver breeding stock.[79] The 3.7 billion chickens consumed annually in the U.S.A. come from breeding stock controlled by some 15 primary breeders.[80]

In 1988 Shaver Poultry was sold by Cargill Ltd. to Institut de Séléction Animale (Mérieux Group) of France. "Cargill has concluded that poultry breeding is out of the mainstream of its integrated poultry operations. Cargill will concentrate future resources on live production, processing and marketing of poultry products. . . . Cargill has major poultry production, processing and marketing operations in Argentina, Honduras, the United Kingdom and the United States."[81]

The simplifications that we are most apt to overlook, because they are so obvious, are the elimination of the mixed, or diversified, farm and its replacement by a commercial monoculture production unit managed by a professionally trained "agriculturalist", accompanied by a reduction in the number of farmers and the consolidation of farms.

In earlier chapters we have observed these manifestations of the logic of simplification, but observing the consequences alone can induce the kind of passivity or fatalism that such simplification desires. Therefore it is necessary to probe more deeply, to explore the inner character of this logic, its history, and the sources of its power. Why is *Science and Technology* imbued with almost mystical authority in our culture today? Why is it appropriate to be cynical about politics, opportunistic about career paths, and ideologically rigid about economics? Why is the destructive course of industrial agriculture pursued as the only possible choice lying between us and starvation while millions go hungry? Or, as Langdon Winner puts it:

> Why has a culture so firmly based upon countless sophisticated instruments, techniques, and systems remained so steadfast in its reluctance to examine its own foundations? Much of the answer can be found in the astonishing hold the idea of "progress" has exercised on social thought during the industrial age. In the 20th century it is usually taken for granted that the only reliable sources for improving the human condition stem from new machines, techniques, and chemicals.[82]

REDUCTIONISM

In the philosophy of science, the idea that the whole is nothing but the sum of its parts, and that the project of science is to understand and explain the universe in terms of its essential parts, is called *reductionism*. It claims that matter can be reduced to a catalogue of its components. This philosophy of science can also be described as linear. A line is simply a series of points, or the sum of a number of points or dots. A line is described in terms of its length, which is the total of the units of measurement: so-many millimetres or kilometres. Linear science consists of adding up the bits to find out how long the line is and observing the direction it is taking. The relationships between the parts can be described in numerical and spatial, though static, terms. Reductionist science consists of determining the size and number and spatial configuration of the constituent parts of the universe and its contents.

Progress, which we often understand as growth, is another expression of this linear logic. If history, culture, and life are linear, then it is natural for us to make assumptions about progress, to insist that the line will not end with us, but be carried forward by us. Like progress, *forward* is a word that creeps in because of our self-centredness or anthropomorphism. *Backward* is a moral pejorative, so we naturally describe the direction that we are going in, the continuation of our line, as forward, or progress. Progress, then, is a moralization of linearity.

The continuous flow phenomenon discussed in Chapter 8 is a literal expression of linearity. So is distancing, which is simply lengthening the line, both in time and space. Likewise, concentration of control requires a hierarchical, linear structure. Monoculture, too, is linear in its essential logic. My own desire to see perfectly straight rows of a crop in field barren of any confusion is an expression of this same linearity.

While it may be obvious that linearity is essentially reductionist, it is less obvious that it is also determinist. If science, indeed Creation, is linear, then our only choice is to find our place in the line. If the whole is the sum of its parts, and we are only a part, then our existence is validated only when we accept our given role in society, the whole. This proper role is itself, according to reductionist logic, determined by the sum of our determinative parts, our genes. Since we inherit these, according to this view of science, in a linear manner from our forebears, we have no choice. Therefore if we are obedient to the natural laws (some may prefer to say, for the sake of their self-respect, if we observe the natural laws) we will take our place without objection in the line-up of life. Those ahead of us are clearly superior, and those behind clearly inferior. We will be rewarded accordingly as winners or losers.

The trickle-down theory of development follows this logic. The theory is based on a hierarchical model of society. Development begins at the top with those most likely to adopt new ways (adapt to an alien culture) or new technology, and to take advantage of new opportunities, or of their neighbours. Aid goes to those who will make best use of it, the entrepreneurs who are already at the top, whether by reason of skill, inheritance, or opportunism. Development will then flow down the social structure, according to the theory. Imagine a long line of people waiting in line at the village well. The most efficient or successful is at the head of the line with the bucket. He drinks what he wants and passes the bucket back to the next in line, and so on. This is trickle-down. Or one could take the case of a well put on the rich man's land by an international aid agency, or the World Bank, because he is the one most likely to take full advantage of the water. Once his crops have been irrigated, what water is left will flow down to the next, and so on. This is actually the situation in many places where development aid has been given as if there were no class or social structure.

Socio-biology is a fairly recent extension of reductionist logic. It projects personal determinism onto the whole of society: the biology of the organism is the biology of the society. Not only is our own self determined by our genes, which are inherited, so also is society determined by the persons, the genes, that constitute it. Thus there is no significant personal or social freedom.

SCIENCE SUPPLANTS THEOLOGY

In spite of the varieties of theories and interpretations of reality available to us, theoretical and creative science seems to have had depressingly little impact on the ideology of commercial science.

In the course of the history of applied science, religion has yielded its authority to science, and science has been largely content to accept an authoritarian role in an otherwise secular society. Many would claim that science now serves the social purposes of medieval religion in the creation of a new feudalism.

Réné Descartes (1596-1650) is generally credited with inaugurating this philosophical orientation. He advocated inductive reasoning; reasoning that proceeds from the particular to the general, from the parts to the whole. Isaac Newton (1642-1727 – Newtonian physics) and others carried this line of reasoning forward and developed reductionist science as the dissection of Creation, the reduction of life to its identifiable bits and pieces, the character of the whole then being induced from a description of its parts and the laws governing their relationships. God as the great watchmaker emerged: the universe could be understood by taking the clock apart and identifying its component parts. God was attributed as the force that made the rules, put it all together and wound it up.

Of course the acceptance of this situation did not go quite so smoothly. Civil and religious authorities alike felt threatened by the new definitions of reality and appealed to their Divine Right: God the clockmaker had put them in their positions of authority in order to ensure the continued functioning of the great clock and to maintain social order, the maintenance of order always being regarded as a divinely granted responsibility, at least by those benefitting from the order maintained.

But the sword of reductionist science was two-edged. Instead of secularism being contained by the ecclesiastical authorities, the new rationalism found it logical to marginalize God on the one hand while on the other revolutionaries claimed authority for their actions as being the expression of the divine intent. While such conflicts have often led to bloody battles and exterminations, the 19th century was more polite. A compromise was worked out to the apparent benefit of both science and religion.

The release of science from the moral and political constraints of religion occurred as Natural Theology, most notably within the state Church of England, evolved in parallel with evolutionary science out of the Revealed Religion of earlier years.

The debate about religion, evolution and the autonomy of nature began in earnest with the publication in 1798 of Thomas Malthus' *Essay on the Principle of Population.* (Darwin's *On the Origin of Species by Means of Natural Selection* was not published until 1859.) Malthus held that population growth was bound to outstrip food production, resulting in periodic famine. (Population, unchecked, was bound to grow geometrically while at best the food supply could only grow arithmetically.) This was the basis for the doctrine of the survival of the fittest that emerged later.

Wm. Paley, a contemporary of Malthus and, like Malthus, a Church of England (Anglican) cleric, is credited with laying the theological foundations for theological reductionism. In the tradition of Descartes, Paley observed only the glory of God in the wonders of Creation as illuminated by science. His Natural Theology reassured those who felt their universe threatened by the new science that their world was in good hands, and that scientific discovery would only magnify the power and glory of the Creator. Nevertheless, during the latter half of the 19th century the relationship between science and theology changed as secularism sought to make the claims of theology so abstract that they could not come into conflict with the discoveries of science.

The doctrine of the survival of the fittest, while popularly attributed to Malthus and/or Darwin, was actually put forward by of one of Darwin's contemporaries, Herbert Spencer, whose extremist interpretation of Malthus became the foundation of Social Darwinism, and later, socio-biology.

Like Malthus, Darwin did not view his work as antagonistic to theology or the church, and while the "controversy in the 19th century between science and theology was very heated indeed . . . at another level the protagonists in that debate were in fundamental agreement. They were fighting over the best ways of rationalizing the same set of assumptions about the existing order."[83]

As science assumed an increasingly autonomous orientation, the theologians attempted to maintain that all was well. The final result, however, was not what they would have wished. In retrospect, we could say of the first half of the 19th century that the church baptized and then confirmed Science, and Science, like an adolescent, then left the church, not only empowered, but filled with pride. The church, for its part, had given over any critical relationship to Science: "the view of God changed from a natural theology of harmony in nature and society . . . to a Deity identified with the self-acting laws of nature. The latter were laws of progress through struggle. . . . Science did not replace God: God became identified with the laws of nature."[84]

In the meantime, the practitioners of Science were not content to be confined to the laboratories of the universities. They had ventured forth into the commercial realm of applied science, technology, and were finding their rewards not in the blessings of the church, but in the gains of the marketplace.

Spencer's theory of the survival of the fittest, "became a rationale for unfettered capitalism, imperialism, and racism."[85] There is a strong argument to be made that British imperialism and the class structure of capitalism both owe a profound debt of gratitude not only to Adam Smith, but to Malthus, Paley, and the other Natural Theologians of the 19th century who provided the rationalization so necessary to the maintenance of social order in the face of exploitation. The Social Darwinists became the missionaries of capitalism, extolling the benefits of what, to them, was necessity. That the spread of the market economy required the force of the state was not a deterrent to their enthusiasm, just as today gigantic state subsidies to the corporate sector are no deterrent to the proclamation of the gospel of free enterprise. On the other side, all attempts at reform of inequities and injustices could be dismissed as in defiance of Nature and its laws.

There is little practical difference between yielding to the laws of Nature and saying that "it's all in the genes." Either way, it is our lot in life to find and accept our place in the natural order of things. Science devotes itself to illuminating this natural order while technology is the inevitable expression of our efforts to organize our daily life according to the natural laws. Hence the union of Science and Technology that is so widely propagated today. If there is a God, God has been marginalized to the role of therapist, or solace in the face of the Inevitable, for which God, too, is responsible as the Creator of these iron laws. Thus the church is not to meddle in politics, economics, or science, and is to be content to preoccupy itself with debates on sexual mores and morality, rather than the life and death issues of an economic system which increases the wealth and power of an elite at the expense of those it deprives while ravaging Creation.

> If one accepts biological determinism, nothing need be changed, for what falls in the realm of necessity falls outside the realm of justice. The issue of justice arises only when there is choice.[86]

DETERMINISM

Although the emergence of micro-biology and genetic engineering in the last decade has reinforced the determinism of 19th century social-Darwinism, it is also spawning new visions and interpretations of the character of the universe, interpretations that are at last challenging the reductionist model of what is scientifically and socially observed and experienced. Science, attempting to gain a more profound understanding of the "laws of nature", is offering other paradigms. One such paradigm is the *self-organising* or *process* system:

> Perhaps the most crucial feature of self-organising systems is what mathematicians call nonlinearity. For 300 years, scientists have largely been preoccupied with linear systems. . . . A linear system is said to be nothing more than the sum of its parts. . . . By contrast, a nonlinear system is more than the sum of its parts. . . . In reality, all physical systems are nonlinear, but they may behave in an approximately linear way when close to equilibrium. Traditionally, scientists tended to treat complex systems as annoying aberrations. Nonlinear systems are harder to study than linear ones. By focusing attention on simple linear systems, science developed a strongly reductionist flavour. . . . We are beginning to see complexity as a natural state of affairs, rather than as an aberration.[87]

COMPLEXITY

If reductionism results in linear science, which pursues simplification, then complexity must be a sign of failure to get to the truth. If the process is complex, then it cannot be scientific. The food system pursues this logic: polyculture is reduced to monoculture; the mixed farm becomes specialised; the art of feeding livestock, or the earth, or our own babies, is reduced to a scientific formula determined *outside* of the system in which it is to be utilized: Shaver Poultry in Cambridge, Ontario, regularly calculates the most economical feed ration for its chicks wherever they are, from the Philippines to Africa, dispatching the advice electronically. Cargill will be happy to advise the farmer of which feed is best for her animals according to the formulas worked out in its corporate lab many miles away, if not in another country.

The food system is similarly simplified in structure: wholesalers and processors become one, and the whole market is streamlined so that it can be centrally controlled. The appearance of a multitude of so-called independent retailers masks the fact that they almost all have supply contracts with one of a small handful of franchisors or wholesalers. The same thing holds true on the farm where, as already noted, six or seven corporations supply almost all agricultural inputs.

The present neo-conservative ideological culture that proclaims the holy trinity of efficiency, productivity, and competitiveness cannot, of course, follow its own rules. The universe simply does not function in terms of such simplistic slogans.

Ecologically, the survival of the fittest requires diversity and complexity. Life processes depend on the constant interaction between organism and environment, and on each being changed by the other in this dialectical process. Over-adaptation and simplification lead to the graveyard, as the organism becomes over-specialized and unable to interact with its changing environment. As an editorial in the U.S. journal *Science* put it: "Some of our crop varieties require human assistance for survival."[87]

For all its claims to being scientific, and rational, the global food system has become irrational and regressive. There has been a steady overpowering of diversity and complexity by the technology of simplification and uniformity, despite the consequences. This

> ...requires not only a theory of direction but also a moral judgement. ... The shibboleths of progressivism are the superiority of man in the cosmos, of industrial man in the world economy, and of liberal democratic man in world society. We have, then, a kind of Whig biology, which sees all of evolution as leading to entrepreneurial man.[88]

The President of Northern Telecom, in a speech, advised that, "If we are to sustain our standard of living, then we must take definitive steps to keep our country in a position of technological strength . . . with an entrepreneurial culture."[89]

If biological survival and human community depend on complexity and diversity, we must begin to rethink the paradigms of our food system, and its principles of organization and behaviour.

CHAPTER 13

REVERSING
THE LOGIC

Those who benefit well from the current food system and political economy would like us all to believe that we inhabit, if not the best, then the only possible of all worlds. Using the food system as an example, I have described the logic of our industrial political economy. The forms of our food system, from the computer and the supermarket to biotechnology, the Green Revolution, and capital intensive monoculture, are all expressions of Cartesian reductionist philosophy joined with social-Darwinist science.

Given the growing number of soup kitchens and food banks at home ("35,000 kids depend on food charity" reads the Christmastime headline of a Toronto newspaper) and starvation abroad, it is hard to concede that our present Market Economy is either the best or the only possible way to organize the distribution of resources, goods and services essential to our life together.

> [In the past three years] hundreds of thousands of the developing world's children have given their lives to pay their countries' debts, and many millions more are still paying the interest with their malnourished minds and bodies.[90]

Envisioning alternatives is usually dismissed as utopian, but there is nothing more utopian than the idea that our system is adequate, or just, and that we can carry on with it. If we reject the infinite projection of our present food system into the future, then we must seek and implement alternatives. I suggest three principles to guide us: *proximity*, *diversity* and *balance*.

PROXIMITY

The principle of proximity is simple: food should be consumed as close to the point and condition of production as possible. Maximum nutritional quality, maximum food security, maximum energy efficiency, and maximum return to those who contribute most to the food production process can be achieved in this way. Proximity has historically been simply a fact of life for most people.

Another way of describing proximity is to say that the closer the food source is to the consumer, the less *money* is required for nutrition. An economic system that seeks to maximize the amount of money that can be made out of anything will pursue the logic of distancing, not proximity. Under the logic of proximity, there is very limited opportunity for chemical, mechanical, technological, or speculative intervention, since the objective is to minimize, not maximize, cash flow.

We are beginning to become aware of the extent to which distancing enables us to obscure the impact or fall-out of our food system. The ecological consequences of clearing rain forests for short-term cheap beef production, the consequences of over-fishing with deep-sea factory-freezer trawlers, the erosion of land resulting from continuous corn production, and the pollution of our sources of water through the gradual leaching of agricultural chemicals have been all but invisible in our short-sightedness. I remember vividly the gully in the hillside of continuous-corn beside the highway to town (Truro, N.S.). Year by year it got deeper and wider and each year the farmer had to make larger detours around it to cultivate and plant his corn. Finally the farmer had to dump tons of rock into it to fill it up to make the field usable, but no longer for corn. The fine clay soil was long gone downstream.

Proximity makes it difficult to avoid or obscure the consequences of what we do, whether it is the production and disposal of garbage or the overuse and pollution of water sources. For example, the overuse of surface water is obvious very quickly, while the overdrawing of water from an aquifer hundreds of feet below ground will not be apparent for some time. Cubans are aware that if they draw too much water from the aquifer under their island the sea water will enter the aquifer, making the watersource unusable. In contrast, the water table under Saudi Arabia is dropping at a rate of up to 45 metres per year in some places, with 92% of that water used for irrigating the desert in order to produce wheat while their water source is increasingly contaminated with sea water.

In the same way, water pollution from surface run-off of manure will be apparent very quickly, while the pollution from subtle agro-toxins may not be apparent for years. The irrigation of crops can be a form of distancing, the distance being overland through long pipes so that those who benefit in the short term are not aware that the lake is going dry. The alternative is better management of the water that is nearby, and this may require a transformation in the way we see the world. During the 1988 drought a prairie grain farmer explained to me how there used to be sloughs and water holes on the land his grandfather broke, but surface water gradually came to be defined as a problem to be gotten rid of as increasingly larger equipment was used. The sloughs and wet holes – the natural reservoirs – had fallen into the same category as weeds, a nuisance to gotten rid of and a competitor for the land needed to grow a crop. Unfortunately it may take more than one drought to change our thinking so that we understand water as a resource to be conserved.

Proximity obviously eliminates the demand that long-distance transportation makes on food for durability and shelf-life. Under a regime of proximity there is no need to design a tomato whose primary characteristic is durability. Nutrition can be the paramount concern. The demands of proximity on potato production would mean growing varieties that were suitable to the local conditions and would provide maximum nutrition over a long harvest period, rather than suitability for simultaneous harvesting and processing into frozen french fries being the major criterion for what is grown and where and how. Proximity applied to other vegetables would mean the production of hardy local crops like apples, carrots, and cole crops (cabbages, Brussels sprouts, etc.) that store well in a good cold cellar without processing or packaging.

Of course, the more seriously proximity was taken as an organizing principle, the more impact it would have on demographics. Human settlement should be guided by the availability of food, as was the case historically for most people, rather than assuming that it is reasonable to haul food thousands of kilometres overland, or to fly it by jet halfway around the world, to feed a population centre *because it is there.* This simply makes too many demands on the food itself and imposes too many distortions on the food system. We might have to seriously consider decentralizing human settlements rather than continue to assume that our current limitless centralization is the only possible way we can live together. Accompanying this would have to be the repopulation of rural towns and villages. This, in turn, would raise the social question of what kind of human settlements we really want and what kind are really sustainable. Food would have to be reintegrated into culture instead of marginalized as commodity.

The requirement that all cities produce 50% or more of their vegetable requirements within their city limits would have drastic and healthy consequences. It would have parallel consequences for those areas of the world presently under duress to produce and sell food to us so that we can continue to live as we do. If we were to grow much more of our own food near to home, then farm labourers, landless peasants, and peasant farmers around the world would stand a better chance of being able to feed themselves and their own communities. Brazilian peasants would not be pushed off the good land, so that a TNC can grow soybeans for export to feed European cattle, and forced onto marginal hill or forested land that should not be cultivated. Cassava would not be grown in Thailand to produce tapioca for export to Europe by a TNC such as Cargill as a high-protein feed supplement for livestock.

Proximity is no cure-all, but in conjunction with other principles such as diversity and balance, would require both a radical transformation of the present North American food system and a radically different appreciation of human community. It would also provide society with more meaningful challenges than inventing new technologies to increase the distance between us and our food sources.

DIVERSITY

The pursuit of genetic diversity combined with the criterion of proximity would eliminate a great many pseudo-diverse items from the supermarket shelves while increasing the varieties of locally and regionally grown produce. Instead of two or three varieties of apples, there might be ten, with at least one of them a traditional variety that stores well until spring. The apple tree in our front yard on the farm was at least a century old. Its apples were not fit to eat until after a good hard frost; picked then, they would keep at the top of our cellar stairs until early spring, when the rhubarb was ready to pick.

At the same time such practices would increase our appreciation of traditional polyculture and historic methods of food production while preserving the stock of genetic resources that are essential to a healthy food system and a healthy ecology.

Reductionist logic has greatly eroded our understanding of how processes and relationships create the conditions of community and ecology. Scientifically-designed baby formula administered with a plastic bottle with a rubber nipple is no substitute for a mother's breast. Starting life with a bottle and no cuddling probably has an effect similar to that of eating all your meals at a stand-up counter in a subway station. To meet the criteria of proximity and local production, there is nothing better than a mother's breast.

Fits and starts, trial and error might better describe the unfolding of life and the development of its web than any linear notion of progress. Thus a fungus will send out its "tentacles" in all directions until some of them touch a food source. Then it will withdraw its other exploratory probes and concentrate all of them on the food source. "Its collective organization and indeterminate growth allow it the best of all worlds by switching between sometimes radically different developmental pathways to suit different tasks."[91]

Organic chemistry in life is the outcome of a very long evolution, and it represents a highly restricted assemblage of compounds; incompatible compounds have been eliminated. In my opinion, an organic compound which does not now occur in living things has to be regarded as an evolutionary reject. Simply put, somewhere down the line a few billion years ago, perhaps some living cell got it into its head to synthesize dioxin and has never been heard from since. You need to regard the products of the petrochemical industry as evolutionary misfits and therefore very likely to be incompatible with the chemistry of living things.[92]

In a culture of superficiality, we seem to have substituted numbers for reality. Success is measured by cash flow, and diversity is measured in terms of how many different packaged goods can be produced out of identical raw materials. If reductionist logic is the truth, then reality can be determined by sheer enumeration. The voting lists would then tell you everything there is to know about a village or a city. But we know that is not true. In a large city, knowing that it is three kilometres from point A to point B tells you very little about how long it actually takes to get there by car or public transit, though it may give you a fair idea of how long by foot or bicycle. That is because there are so many other factors that have to be accounted for in the case of using a car or bus. In the same fashion, knowing that you planted 60,000 seeds will tell you just that, not that you will harvest 60,000 plants. There are a great many other factors that must be considered along the way, which is why the food-for-profit system seeks control through monoculture and the reduction of variables by means of industrialization.

While reductionist logic seeks to minimize variables, the result of the apparent stability achieved in, say, a plant population, is vulnerability. The greater the uniformity, the greater the vulnerability, the greater the dependency, the greater the insecurity. If the fans are not turned on at the right time in the chicken barn, a catastrophe will result. Chickens are not normally so dependent. If hybrid corn does not receive the right amount of the required pesticides and fertilizer, or a new bug wanders by, the whole crop is at risk because there is no diversity. If a bug strikes one, it strikes all in a monoculture.

A few years ago the Canadian Agricultural Chemicals Association changed its name to the Canadian Crop Protection Institute. Public distrust of chemicals and chemical agriculture was growing, and "crop protection" was a more comforting idea. But the name change also signalled the increasing dependency of industrial agricultural crops on "protection". No longer able to make their way in the natural world on the basis of their own strengths, industrial crops are dependent on an army of external interventions for their survival. In the case of agricultural chemicals, dependency has grown so extreme that the protection fails: "hostile" bugs develop their own defenses in the form of immunity to the chemicals which are supposed to be protecting the plants. The chemical companies respond by continuously designing plants capable of tolerating higher levels of pesticide or tolerating other pesticides the bugs are not yet immune to.

A sustainable food system must reduce its dependency on external supports to a minimum, and this can be achieved by maximizing *diversity* so that the food system as a whole is interdependent. Genetic diversity is the basis of a healthy population. It provides the resources to respond to and interact with a constantly changing environment. If one variety succumbs, there will be another that won't, and a new resistance will be acquired.

The recognition of diversity as the basis of a healthy population would demand the reverse of the processes at work in our food system. We would know that we could not export what worked for us as the answer to a problem elsewhere. We would seek to expand the genetic base of our nutrition and look for heterogeneity rather than uniformity. But this would be not only in genetic resources. The same logic would apply to processing in a decentralized system, and to the ways of preserving and distributing food. If diversity is of any significance, then the least desirable way to organize our food supply is to centralize the control over it into the hands of five or six mega-corporations.

BALANCE

Linear processes are incapable of balance. *Balance* implies some equation between two or more participants, and to be sustainable, there must also be justice. In the case of a sustainable and just food system, the balance must exist between those who grow the food and those who prepare it, between those who distribute it and those who eat it. There must be some balance between the re- sources used to produce the food and the replenishing of those resources. "Continuous flow" is not the logic of a sustainable or just system, since it implies uni-directional movement. Phosphate rock mined in Florida and shipped to Ontario, applied to farm land along with herbicides produced from Alberta oil in Windsor, On- tario, in order to grow corn that is then shipped to Nova Scotia to feed livestock that is shipped back to Montreal, does not add up to a balanced system. In the same way, there is no balance in a food system that requires its primary producers, as a rule, to live on a fraction of the income that is appropriated *out of the same system* by the chief executives and senior managers of the corporations that produce the agricultural inputs or process and distribute the food.

There is a perverse logic in the traditional antipathy of farm- ers towards unionized food processing plant workers or grain han- dlers. Perhaps farmers, wedded to an ideology of rugged individu- alism, resent the corporate strength of the unionized workers who may succeed through collective bargaining in getting an adequate wage. But those same farmers, perhaps because they have been indoctrinated to devalue their labour and to see themselves as businessmen, seem less concerned about the salaries of corporate management, or the profits made by the food companies. In other words, there is a characteristic *imbalance* in the allocation of re- turn to labour in the linear food system, and this ought to be chal- lenged by those who are the primary victims of the system.

A system seeks balance, like the sea water entering the aquifer under Cuba. When a hole for a fence post is dug in satu- rated ground, the hole will quickly fill with water and earth if the fence post is not quickly put in and the whole filled.

The idea of balance can also be observed in the determination of plants and animals to reproduce themselves. If a hayfield is left to mature and go to seed, the plants then die back, having fulfilled their purpose. In a temperate climate the cycle is annual. If live- stock are introduced, however, the plants will be grazed before they reach the seeding stage and then will continue to grow, trying to reach that stage again. Cutting a field for hay will produce the same results. However, if the natural annual cycle is interfered with, then responsibility must be taken for maintaining the balance. Thus the livestock will deposit their manure directly, on pasture, or the farmer removing the hay will have to return either the manure or replenish the resource in some other way, as in crop rotation. The only alternative is to construct a linear dependent system.

An unjust, imbalanced system cannot be maintained without life-denying coercion and ecological violence. As we have noted earlier, in many places this force takes the form of death squads which seek to maintain sufficient fear among a deprived population that they will not try to take over the lands that are being withheld from sustenance production, usually in order to produce cash crops for export with the support of a government that seeks to preserve its privileges. It may also be complying with the demands of international finance (IMF/World Bank) to repay the debts incurred in the construction of the unjust, imbalanced system in the first place.

That is why the issue of privatization is important. The essence of private property is the right and the ability to exclude others from the use or enjoyment of that property. Inequities and inequalities are far more easily maintained in a privatized culture than in a cooperative and genuinely balanced economy.

CHAPTER 14

SELF-RELIANT
FOOD SYSTEMS

It is not enough to leave the discussion of a just and sustainable food system resting on the logic of proximity, diversity and balance. We must consider the characteristics of a self-reliant food system incorporating these principles. The real fruits of our labour should be the development of human communities based on ecological sustainability and economic justice.

Self-reliance does not mean isolation or autonomy. It simply means not being dependent on another, that is, *relying* on self, not another, and entering into external economic relations on the basis of equity and mutuality. Self-sufficiency, on the other hand, can be described as an attempt to be self-contained and independent, or autonomous.

BIO-REGIONALISM

Self-reliance requires, *a priori*, a working definition of *self*. In the linear corporate food system we have been describing, the self is a single unit, one piece of the system like any other piece: the self is a consumer or a worker, a means to a profit. In a self-reliant, just, and sustainable food system, the self is defined in a real and specific geographic and biologically based context.

We all live in a particular geographic and biological place. This may seem a rather obvious statement, but our present industrial food system is built on the assumption that we do not live anywhere in particular and have no biological context. Biology and geography are simply natural resources to be exploited. A sustainable food system, by contrast, is by definition rooted in a particular ecology, and since these are all different, there will be many different food systems, even though they may share many common features. These particular places are bio-regions: specific biological and geographical material locations.

The nation-state is considered the basic unit of an economy, even though very few nation-states bear any more than a casual or accidental relationship to a bio-region. Most nation-states by their very structure and size overpower or simply exclude any bio-regionalism. Both Canada and the United States are good examples of this. Cuba, on the other hand, might be considered a bio-region, while Japan might be considered a federation of several bio-regions conforming with its islands.

Consider that rivers have always been arteries of societies, the thoroughfare around or along which communities have been built. Yet imperialism has almost always chosen rivers as boundary lines because they offer one of the few lines of demarcation that can be easily identified. If territory is to be defended, it helps to be able to tell the army where it is.

Similarly commerce, left to follow its own particular interests, will locate around a lake, or on a coastline, not in the middle of a landmass. The reason is simple: water is the cheapest and most sustainable means of transportation.

There are natural, geographical ways of describing bio-regions, but it is less by their boundaries, which militarily may well be exasperatingly vague, than by their character. For example, the Great Plains of North America does not have clear boundaries that conform to those drawn up using the Mississippi River as a border. Nor does the political boundary of the 49th parallel bear any natural relationship to the Great Plains. Nor do the political divisions of the maritime provinces of Canada and the U.S.A. – New Brunswick, Maine, and Nova Scotia – bear much resemblance to the natural boundaries of the region. (Prince Edward Island and

Newfoundland have to be considered separately because each is primarily its own bio-region before it is anything else.) The mountain-defined West Coast – British Columbia and half of Alberta – constitute a bio-region which includes much of Washington state and even Oregon.

Bio-regionalism is *not* the same as continentalism. There is little hope of ecologically-sound or geographically-based economies in a political unit of the size and character of the U.S.A. or the Canada/U.S.A. that "free trade" has accomplished. The Maritime provinces and New England states have discovered that just as heavy industry was located in their region in the last century, it can be relocated elsewhere when it serves certain interests, interests that are not those of *any* particular region. Thus, if one speaks of bio-regions that cross political boundaries, then it is also necessary to draw political boundaries around sustainable regions. The political map of the U.S.A., and many other countries, would have to change drastically.

Bringing about such political change is obviously dependent on a radical change in the political and economic forces. Here I am only trying to establish the guidelines for self-reliance, particularly with regard to food, upon which such a change would have to be based.

There is nothing magic about bio-regions. If, however, one is going to consider an economy, and a culture, that is based on material reality rather than political or ideological abstractions, then one has to begin with a description and assessment of the material base. Sustainable food production requires it.

Decentralized bio-regional control is essential to an ecological economy. The possibility of face-to-face communication and a common sense of place (proximity) may, in fact, be essential to any healthy political unit.

Such criteria, however, bring us into immediate conflict with current population policies or practices. In the Market Economy it is expected that people will move to where there are jobs. If there are jobs to be had in Toronto, Maritimers are expected to move there to fill them, regardless of such factors as wage levels for the available jobs, housing, or air quality. Market Economy theory regards labour as nothing more than one of the factors of production, and thus it must be as free to move as capital or services. The conflict with restrictive immigration policies is obvious. "Free trade" in services should include free movement of labour if it is to be consistent.

One of the most visible and violent consequences of the industrialization of the food system has been its effect on rural communities, including both infrastructure and population. The closing down of rail branch lines and grain elevators, milk routes and machinery dealers, schools and community services, referred to as "rationalization" in current political jargon, has destroyed the viability of rural communities from coast to coast. Given the values of the Market Economy and the primacy it gives to the accumulation of capital, this is perfectly logical, but it runs counter to any notion of sustainability. People need to live in a community not only for social and commercial services, but also for their nurture and growth. While individual farm bankruptcy is bad, the failure of a community is even more devastating since it eliminates the context within which personal grief can be borne and shared and within which a different life can be nurtured. But even without putting it in these extreme terms, the isolation imposed on farming people by the current industrial, capital-intensive system makes it both unattractive and dehumanizing. Farm children know this very well, and while they may feel real regret at the choice they make, they choose not to carry on on the farm not because they do not like the work, but because they cannot tolerate the isolation and lack of community.

Clearly, then, any move towards bio-regionalism and sustainability must involve a deliberate population policy: a policy of repopulation of rural communities. This may mean establishing new rural communities that are bio-regionally based, rather than rebuilding communities that were situated according to the dictates of the railways or foreign commercial interests and not according to the needs of the land and the people.

There is little new in all this. In other lands and at other times, people have lived, and continue to live, in villages while working the surrounding land.[93] While there have been both good and bad reasons for this, the pattern remains a sound one. But given the expectations people are now raised with, both good and bad, the isolated village is not enough. A good public transportation system that can provide access to larger centres with the cultural and intellectual resources that require a larger population base is both reasonable and necessary. While we may have convinced ourselves that the private automobile provides maximum freedom of movement, it does so only for those of certain ages and physical abilities, and only then at very high cost. Universal accessibility, meaning children and seniors, disabled and healthy, without regard to income, should be the criterion of public transportation just as it should be for nutrition.

It may, in fact, be appropriate that the rail lines are being abandoned, if only to show how badly they are needed, though perhaps organized and built to sustain a healthy society rather than to export its resources.

TRADE

Self-reliance, as we have noted, is not the same as self-sufficiency. While it may be possible to achieve a high level of food self-sufficiency in some locations, for reasons of cultural and social diversity and experience it may not be desirable. We are left, then, to consider the question of the nature of non-dependent economic relations.

The current ideological climate stresses the importance of organizing an economy around export. A national economy is measured by its balance of trade, and comparative advantage is proclaimed as the golden rule of economic activity. Trade is confused with export. A trading economy is not the same as an export economy: trade is built on reciprocity and equity, while simple export is based on advantage, and taking advantage, getting more than it gives in an imbalanced fashion. Mercantilism, imperialism, and capitalism have all sought gain at the expense of others. Trade, on the other hand, should be understood as a function of communities, while export alone is a function of dependency and domination.

For example, trade between the Maritime region of Canada and the U.S. and the Caribbean could be a trade in potatoes, colecrops, meat, and livestock in exchange for tropical vegetables and fruits. Fish, a high-value product, could be traded between the Maritime region and inland industrial regions for tools and equipment. Trade between bio-regions could be trade of Prairie grains for Ontario (or Minnesota) fruits and vegetables, or Maritime meat for Cuban fruit.

INCLUSIVE ACCOUNTING

A third aspect of self-reliance must be inclusive accounting: accounting that takes account of everything relevant. On a bio-regional base, this means that all costs of infrastructure must be accounted for, as well as resource depletion and labour exploitation. Contemporary accounting practices, reflecting the logic of corporate capitalism, are a negation of this principle because they endeavour to externalize as many costs as possible, assigning them either to future generations, the public purse, or people lying outside their jurisdiction.

A pulp-mill that obtains electrical power that is subsidized by the public, that utilizes and pollutes a public water supply, that pays less for stumpage, or for wood, than the full cost of obtaining that wood and reproducing the forest, is engaged in fraudulent accounting if these factors are externalized and do not appear on the corporate books as part of the costs of doing business.

The same thing holds true for farming and fishing. A factory freezer-trawler that overfishes, thereby reducing the future fish stocks, must be charged for the cost of rebuilding the fish stocks. The social costs for the coastal villages that are deprived of the fish stocks that were the basis of their economy – costs such as unemployment insurance, relocation costs, loss of tax base – must also be included in the costs of operating factory freezer-trawlers, just as the soil losses and pollution resulting from crop monoculture must be charged as costs against the value of the crop.

In the same way, the unpaid wages of farm families and peasant labour must be factored into the cost of exported food. If the wages of the farm worker are not very close to those of the industrial worker who eats the food produced by that labour, the full cost of that food is not being paid, regardless of claims about comparative advantage.

In a bio-regional self-reliant food economy, the human community will insist that all costs must be accounted for, not only the costs of sustainable production, but the costs of community. Sustainability and long-term viability are simply not possible if real costs are externalized and unaccounted for.

SUSTAINABILITY

Self-reliance requires sustainability. It cannot be assumed that fuelwood can be obtained outside the region once all the trees are gone at home. Self-reliance is the negation of export monoculture and dependency on imported food or agricultural inputs.

Sustainability means that there is no time limit to the economy. Sustainable food production means that present production is not being obtained at the expense of future production. This is not to say that it is a static system because biology itself is not static. In a sustainable food system, like a balanced equation, there may be continuous substitution of one factor for another and for increasing some while decreasing others. Fish species and food crops may well vary as other factors vary – such as long-term weather patterns, water levels, population pressures and deliberate or natural selection of species and varieties – not only from place to place but from generation to generation.

Sustainability also means that the resources called upon, or used, are renewed by the very process that calls upon them. If we are going to eat the progeny of a cow, then provision must also be made for the reproduction of that cow. If cereal crops are eaten, provision must be made for sufficient seed to be saved to replant the crop next season.

Biological sustainability, like any economy, requires diversity. All organisms (and an economy is an expression of a population of organisms) require genetic diversity in order for the species to be able to evolve with the evolving environment. Hybrid corn does not breed true. It degenerates and is unable to survive, having traded long-term survival for short-term, unsustainable productivity.

The comparative advantage of monoculture is deceptive: it does not reckon on a future. It is biologically static and consequently dependent. Without external inputs it must die. It cannot propagate itself reliably, and is subject to all sorts of attacks for which it has few internal defenses.

Complexity and diversity are the keys to biological health and security, and bio-regions are the site of integrated and sustainable diversity. The external imposition of uniformity, whether to make harvesting easier, storage possible, or to facilitate corporate management, has its price. The price of uniformity is vulnerability and dependency.

To be sustainable, the system must also be basically *organic*, that is, based on what occurs within the local ecosystem naturally, not dependent on externally produced inputs or support systems such as chemical fertilizer or "crop protection" materials (chemically or biologically fabricated agro-toxins), whether produced locally or brought into the bio-region from outside sources. It means relying on the natural systems that have evolved over very long periods of time, during which organisms and components have interacted and reproduced on a continuing basis without dependency on foreign or imported inputs, including engineered genes.

To describe a self-reliant food system as organic is simply to observe that what is non-organic (that is, introduced from outside the natural cycle) generally does not contribute to the health of the organism. The human body has to filter out and dispose of all the foreign matter that is introduced into its nutrient intake for purposes other than to feed the body. If crops are sprayed with an insecticide that leaves a residue, the human body has to cope with the result of an intervention made in order to make the production of the crop more profitable, but not more sustainable or more nutritious.

A SELF-RELIANT FOOD ECONOMY

All of these factors can be combined in a self-reliant food system that is organically, bio-regionally, and community based. It will mean seasonality in foods, more labour input in production and processing, and greater genetic diversity with a great deal less superficial diversity. Instead of following the divisive and destructive logic of industrial capitalist food, this food system will follow the decentralizing and integrating logic of diversity and interaction and the nurturing of biological and human communities.

This must mean smaller production units, smaller and more locally designed equipment, and the recycling of nutrients and organic matter, from air and water to manure and garbage. It must also mean a vastly reduced role, if any, for transnational chemical companies and international grain speculators and traders. At the public or consumer end, it would probably mean the break-up of the vast food processing and distributing conglomerates now operating, as processing and packaging are reduced and the whole food system decentralized and localized. Fruits and vegetables are simply most nutritious when they are fresh-picked. They have no choice but to deteriorate rapidly, since once harvested they are living organisms removed from their life-support systems. The most direct route, the least distance, to the final eater is the best route.

CHAPTER 15

DOWN TO EARTH

The Market Economy culture, with its accompanying technological determinism, is now so widespread and so deeply entrenched that it is hard to even conceive of things being otherwise. The assumption that an economy, to deliver the goods, has to be based on greed and individualism appears to gain strength daily. The language of profit and efficiency, technology and competition, spreads through the media and distorts our vocabulary so that it is increasingly difficult to even find the words through which a different vision might be expressed. While we may recognize the deepening ecological crisis, at the same time we sense our own alienation from the creation that sustains us. While we have profound myths and histories to draw upon, as well as ancient visions, our imagination appears to have atrophied and our nerve withered.

To envision a radical alternative to the Market Economy that would meet the requirements of Biblical faith, ecological sustainability, and human community is not utopian. It is utopian to think that we can solve the problems of the growing destruction of Earth's resources, increasing hunger and deprivation, and deepening concentration of wealth and power in the hands of a tiny fraction of the world's people, with more debt, more technology, more oppression, and yet more exhortation to be competitive and productive.

In this book I have deliberately worked at two levels: theory and concrete analysis. When moving into the future, the same dialectic is essential. Taking small, specific steps toward an inclusive economy of food will at the same time nurture the vision that directs those steps. We cannot wait for a revolution to begin creating a new society: too much life is already being destroyed and too many options eliminated, as in the destruction of tropical rainforest and the loss of genetic diversity. The revolution begins with the ability to imagine a different future.

UNIVERSAL ACCESS TO NUTRITION

It is strange how we have come to regard as normal and reasonable the notion that the only way to eat is to first buy food at a store. We don't start life this way, and it is often a matter of years before we learn how to function properly as customers in the food system.

The Biblical story of the manna in the wilderness and the Christian sacrament of the Eucharist, as described in Chapter 2, are expressions of a different economy, an economy of universal access. We are encouraged by Market Economy ideology to dismiss this vision and to require people to buy their basic nutrition, not because it is good for them, but because it commits them to the economy of profit.

If we were to be consistent and the Market Economy universal, we might carry with us little air meters, so we could pay for the air we require. It would be a little complicated, because we would have to have accounts with "owners" of the air in every jurisdiction through which we might pass. Truly a challenge to the electronics and information processing engineers! But buying our basic nutrition with money is no less absurd, though it does accurately reflect the ethics of an economy which measures success in terms of accumulated capital and value in terms of price.

If to be alive is to do more than simply make money, then we must consider how we can make it possible to think of our lives differently. The provision of, or allowance for, the minimal requirements of air, water, and food for everybody is a commonsense beginning. The issue is universal rather than market access. Applied to a food system, this would simply mean that the economy of nursing mother and baby would be taken as normative, not exceptional. (The manufacturers of infant formula, baby foods, and now "weaning foods" have waged a determined campaign against breast feeding in order to enlarge their market while subverting the non-market economy.)

There are many ways one can imagine organizing the production and distribution of food to ensure that every person receives what they require as members of the community. Children do not make a decision to be born. We bring them into the world, and they remain our responsibility. In a sense we have recognized this in Canada through our medicare system with its principle of universal access. Yet basic health care, in the form of good nutrition, remains in the competitive Market Economy. The challenge now is to extend the already-accepted logic of sick-care to the provision of food. If our socialized medicine included nutrition, one of the ancillary benefits would certainly be the reduction of our sick-care costs.

For a start, it ought to be possible for anyone who is ill because they are malnourished to get a prescription for food, just as they would get a prescription for a drug if that were what they needed. If such an idea seems utopian, ask the drug companies if they think prescribing drugs under medicare is a bad idea. The big food companies might love the idea of prescribing food if the public would pay for it.

If generic drugs are a good idea, so then is generic food. So when prescribing, the health professionals could stipulate clean, unprocessed food, and they could ensure that the mark-up would be minimal by simply setting ceiling prices for food, based on full costs of production.

If the supply of clean, generic, just plain, food is inadequate, the health authority could then seek to contract with farmers directly to provide the quantity and quality of food required. This food would then be available in a clinic without charge to those ordered by the health professional to eat better.

Probably it would not be long before the healthy people realized that they were being discriminated against and began to seek the same quality food. They might insist that they had as much right to the public or socialized food as the sick people, and of course they would be right.

Since good health cannot be achieved with sick food, and recognizing that food allergies are an increasing problem, we would want to ensure that the food in an alternative system is also healthy. The production of healthy food would mean, in practice, the production of what is called "organic" food, that is, food produced without artificial fertilizers, pesticides, herbicides, preservatives, etc. It would mean even more than that, because even with the best clean soil, one cannot grow clean produce like lettuce in an environment like that of Toronto: the air is too polluted. This does not mean the requirement is impossible, just that it is more radical than we might initially think.

Just as we have found it necessary to protect the public interest by legislating standards for drugs, we could also legislate standards for food quality, or at least for the food that goes through the public nutrition sector. At the same time, society as a whole would have to pay the primary producers, who should be comparable to the medical profession in public esteem and monetary value, to produce the kind and quality of food we require. This need not raise the cost of food to the society, since this approach would eliminate much costly processing, packaging and advertising, to say nothing of costly agricultural inputs like pesticides and chemical fertilizers.

In accordance with the principle of proximity, the production of clean food would need to be done as close to where the population centres are as possible, thus reducing the present absurd extent of long-distance overland trucking and freeing resources for the primary production of healthy food.

OWNERSHIP

We still have many romantic images of the family farm, but it is essential that we consider what they really are, and whether or not they ever really existed. It may be that "the family farm" is another of those alienating dreams that render us impotent in the face of the forces taking control of the food system. As we rethink the food system, the rapid decline in the number of family farms could be viewed as an opportunity rather than a disaster, encouraging us to recognize that the private ownership of the means of production, including land, may be a major cause of the destruction of those valuable and real elements of the family farm that we value. The profound need for human community, and the real practical need for security of tenure on the land (for both the farmers' and the land's sake) may compel us to create what are, for this culture, novel forms of farm organization, such as co-operatives and land trusts. As a Salvadorean peasant said, returning to her home after being a refugee in Honduras, "It's stupid to look after your land alone. If you get sick it doesn't get harvested. When we work together, if one person gets sick the land is still looked after."

There are three land issues: ownership, stewardship, and security of tenure.

Farmers feel very strongly that they have to *own* the land they farm, even though about 25% of all farmland currently worked is rented or leased. In the culture of North America it has long been taken for granted that the only real security for agriculture lies in the private ownership of land. There is, for good reason in many cases, a profound distrust of absentee ownership (whether it be by agribusiness or by the state) which includes ownership by the state, but this attitude has been and continues to be very costly for farmers.

For example: when we needed to obtain more land for our farm in Nova Scotia, we were delighted that the provincial government had just introduced a program of landbanking. Under this program we were able to make a deal with a retiring farmer whereby the Province would buy the land and lease it to us at a rate commensurate with its agricultural value. We were assured of security of tenure and a fair agricultural rent for as long as we wanted (which turned out to be about 12 years). However, no sooner was this program in place than the Federation of Agriculture began complaining that farmers had to have an option to purchase, which was not in the program we had been happy to take advantage of. (We wanted to work the land, not own it.) So the government responded in a reasonable fashion: they changed the program so that there was an option to buy and changed the rental basis from the agricultural value of the land to the market value. This effectively doubled the rental rate. Fortunately for us, the government honored our rental agreement under the original terms as long as we farmed. In this case, the farm organization destroyed a very good program simply because of the ideological commitment to the "right" to own land.

Yet it is precisely this ideological committment which is bankrupting farms and destroying the family farm. It is the interest on the debt against farm land, built up in the 70s and early 80s, that is the major cause of farm failure in North America, coupled with commodity prices too low to carry this debt. (Food prices should never have to include the cost of buying the farm all over again, once every generation.) And while individual farmers may still hold legal title to the land, the fact is that their mortgages, and thus their security, are held by outside interests, whether the Farm Credit Corporation, a bank, a provincial lending authority or a credit union. In the United States the insurance companies are now among the major land-owners. In many cases, the farmer now has less security of tenure than medieval serfs had: "The medieval serf had been almost the opposite of a property owner: the land had owned *him*. He could not move freely from place to place, and yet he had inalienable rights to the piece of land to which he was attached."[94]

The net financial effect of this situation on the farm economy is that the farm has to be refinanced once every generation. This constitutes an unsustainable drain on the entire rural economy, not just the farm, and it means that real control does not rest finally in the farmers' hands or in the rural community, but in the corporate boardrooms of the metropolis. Paying interest on a farm mortgage is little different than paying for agricultural chemicals. The money leaves the farm and rural economy and eventually inflates the value of urban land and housing. There is no balance.

One way of holding land so that security of tenure could be achieved would be to have all agricultural land held in some form of public trust. Then the rules of tenure would become a public responsibility rather than being the prerogative of urban capital as is the case now. This would force a clarification of roles and responsibilities: those people who wanted to farm could do so, with security of tenure contingent on their cultural practices and care of the land, and those who wanted to speculate would have to find another way to do so. Rent, if any, on the land being farmed could be geared to the value of the sustainable production of the land. The responsibility of the society to the farmers would be to ensure an adequate living, including pension, and a supportive community with the necessary social and economic infrastructure. Ecology, care of the earth, sustainability, all would then be the concerns and responsibility of the whole community.

There is nothing novel, in fact, in this approach. It is gaining increasing acceptance and popularity as a way of conserving forests and ecological diversity in the United States and elsewhere. Without even questioning the moral legitimacy of owning land, one can begin to de-commodify it by removing it from the market. A land trust can be private, such as the Nature Conservancy, or it can be public, like the Saskatchewan land bank once was. And it could be private or public at any level. There is no reason a province or a municipality or a city could not be the land-holding unit. There is adequate precedent in our park system, which a great many people enjoy. (This is not to suggest that there are no issues to be debated about the philosophy of park management, but at least those issues are in the public domain.) Also, there is no reason that farmers could not themselves form a trust, give or sell their land to the trust and then lease or rent it back. The point is that there are many alternative ways of holding land. That so little thought has been given to these as viable options suggests that the issue is less practical than ideological. The development of a just and sustainable food system is going to require addressing both practical and ideological issues, and the very idea of being able to *own* land at all.

The native peoples of North America have never shared the capitalist concept of land ownership, and they have always understood their relationship to the land in religious or spiritual terms. They are not alone in holding that the land simply cannot be owned. Even within European culture and history there have been different concepts of land ownership, and there is ample precedent, for example in the English *strict laws* of the 19th century, for considering land ownership as a trust, requiring stewardship, not exploitation.

It was the practice of the English landed classes after the English civil war deliberately to tie their lands to their families through the legal instrument known as a strict settlement. The arrangement made the living recipient of rents into a mere tenant of his heir. Being, in effect, only stewards for the next generation, the English landlord class prevented itself from taking the short-term view on land-use. Land had always to be passed to the heir in a condition at least as good as before.[95]

If we think about the possible ways of holding land as a common resource and a trust for future generations with stewardship and sustainability as the criteria of use, then we must also think of social structures and institutions that make this possible. Thus we should consider rural communities that are land based, that allow rural people freedom to change vocation and work and to renew themselves and broaden their horizons, while being assured that the community they call home will continue to be a place to which they can return.

Stewardship of the land and sustainable agriculture require human labour. They demand a variety of work that makes it possible for men and women of all ages to participate in the working life of the farm and the community. From reforestation to composting, from seed conservation to breeding, from cooperative building of social facilities to machinery repair, there should be work for all. Labour intensive gardening might well be a more rewarding form of labour for teen-agers than stacking shelves in a supermarket or serving up prefabricated burgers at the local drive-in for minimum wage.

Food could be restored to its rightful and necessary place in the centre of community cultural life through common labour as well as celebrations.

Our present industrial food system, pursuing the logic of distancing, has effectively alienated many people from an active relationship to food in any role other than that of consumers. Any restructuring of the food system will have to deal with and overcome this alienation. If universal accessibility means that everyone is entitled to adequate nutrition as a member of the society, then everyone also has to take some responsibility for the food system in the same way that they have to take responsibility for their health.

FULFILLING THE BIBLICAL VISION

In Chapter 2 I set out my understanding of the Biblical vision of the economy of food. This vision contains neither a lot of analysis nor specific solutions or answers. Basically the Biblical stories convey an understanding of how we are to organize our economy and treat Creation if we seek to live together in peace. The *how* has to do with relationships and attitudes, and insists that these have to be materialized, to become concrete. Faith has to be incarnated, made flesh, in our economic arrangements. We feed each other first with bread, not a stone. This bread conveys our solidarity. To insist that nourishment – salvation – must be purchased is immoral and a sin. It is a denial of life and of community. Restructuring the economy so that its purpose and function is to provide for the essential needs of all, can best begin with the food system. The personal question is, do we seek justice and community, or power and wealth?

In the middle of our farmhouse kitchen was a round solid pine table. Anyone entering the house came directly into the kitchen and invariably sat down at the table. Being round, the table could accommodate many people, and it had no head place. Being in the kitchen, it was also the work-table for the kitchen economy. Food and community were inseparable. It was around that table that many meetings of the sheep producers and our lamb marketing co-operative were held. It was also at that table that for many years, alienated from the local churches, we held a weekly Bible study and Eucharist. Our children, those staying with us, and a neighbour or two were symbolic of the larger community and economy of which our farm was a part. The spiritual and material incarnation of that experience and vision continues to motivate me.

NOTES

1. McCain's executive quoted in Canadian Grocer, Dec. 1989 (MacLean-Hunter, Toronto, monthly)

2. Canadian Agriculture in the Seventies, Report of the Federal Task Force on Agriculture, Ottawa, Dec. 1969

3. L. Curtain, Food Market Commentary, p. 23, Sept. 1988, (Agriculture Canada, quarterly)

4. Dick Dawson, quoted in Western Producer, Nov. 17, 1988 (Saskatchewan Wheat Pool, Saskatoon, weekly)

5. G. Temple, FOOD In Canada, Nov/Dec. 1988 (MacLean- Hunter, Toronto, monthly)

6. FOOD In Canada, June 1987

7. FOOD in Canada, Oct. 1988

8. Exodus 16:13-21, Jerusalem Bible

9. In addition to Ault Foods, Labatt's operating divisions include: Labatt Brewing Co., Johanna Farms (New Jersey dairy), Ogilvie (flour mills), John Labatt Foods, Holiday Juice, Chateau-Gai (wines), and The Sports Network, according to its 1987 annual report.

10. Canadian Grocer, Jan. 1989

11. Interview, 1986

12. "Calgene has at least 9 corporate-funded partnerships. . . . According to Calgene, the 'most commercially significant accomplishment' in the 1987 R & D programme was the successful expression of 'Bromo-Tol' (bromoxynil herbicide tolerance) gene in tobacco and tomato plants (research sponsored by Rhone-Poulenc Agrochimie)" - Development Dialogue, 1988, Dag Hammarskjold Foundation, Sweden, pp. 1-2

13. Dan Morgan, Merchants of Grain, Penguin, 1980, p. 86

14. Cited by F. H. Buttel, in "Agricultural Structure and Energy Intensity", Comparative Rural and Regional Studies No. 1, Univ. of Guelph, 1979. See

also R. Perelman: "Efficiency in Agriculture: the Economics of Energy" in Radical Agriculture, R. Merrill, ed., Harper Colophone 1976

15. Annual Report, 1986, Oshawa Group Ltd.

16. Development Dialogue, p. 97

17. Canadian Grocer, Feb. 1987

18. For example, according to its 1987 Annual Report, Geo. Weston Ltd. includes four principal operating groups: Weston Foods (food processing), Loblaw Companies ltd. (food distribution), Weston Resources (fisheries and forest products), and Weston Research Centre. The Weston Foods operations include: Weston Bakeries, Soo Line Mills, McCarthy Milling, Stroehmann Bakeries, InterBake (Canadian operations sold in 1988), William Nielson, Bowes, and Instant Products.

The easiest way to identify Weston products is by the address on the package: Weston corporate headquarters is located at 22 St. Clair Ave. E., Toronto, though the name on the package may be Sunfresh, No Name, Loblaws, etc.

Loblaw Companies includes: Loblaws Supermarkets, Combined Merchandisers, Zehrmart, Atlantic Wholesalers, National Grocers, Kelly Douglas, Westfair Foods, and U.S. operations. Loblaws appears as Superstores, Loblaws, Mr. Grocer (acquired from Dominion in 1987), and others such as Fortinos Supermarkets (acquired in 1988).

19. Data in Report on Business Magazine, July 1987

20. After-tax profits for all corporations in the food processing industry have grown steadily since 1983. In 1987 net profits increased 32.5% over 1986 to a total of $1.2-billion.

The return on invested capital for food manufacturing corporations having $10-million or more in assets increased from 12.6% in 1986 to 14.4% in 1987, the highest return on investment for food manufacturing in the past decade.

The inventory turnover ratio – the ratio of sales to inventory – increased to 9.2 times in 1987. This means that the inventory turned over nine times in the course of the year. This is an important figure because the businesses like to represent themselves as working on a very low margin. In a sense this is true, but costs are to a great extent fixed (land, buildings, capital) so that the higher the turnover the more goods these costs are spread over. If the asset turnover ratio is 2%, and inventory turnover is 9 times, then the yield per year is 2 x 9, or 18% per year.

The rate of return on invested capital in the food retailing sector for large corporations ($10-m or more in assets) rose from 9.3% in 1986 to 16%

in 1987 (the 1980-86 average was 10.4%) on the basis of an 84.7% gain in after-tax profits to $580-m.

Combination stores (supermarkets) account for 71% of retail food sales, with the cost of goods purchased accounting for 79.3% of retailer operating expenses. Total employment in this sector averages 275,000 workers.

Statistics from Food Market Commentary, Agriculture Canada, Dec. 1988.

21. George Fleischmann, President, Grocery Products Manufacturers Assoc., speaking in Edmonton, Feb. 1986

22. Globe and Mail, Toronto, Sept. 8, 1988

23. Jack Doyle, Altered Harvest, Viking, 1985, contains a 48-page table of Agribusinesses and the Food Chain, giving investments in agriculture, genetics, and biotechnology research. See also Development Dialogue.

24. Financial Post, Report of the Nation, Winter 1988-89

25. Land Stewardship Letter, Stillwater, Minnesota, Fall, 1988

26. Farm Survey 1988 and Farm Credit Statistics 1988, Farm Credit Corporation, Ottawa

27. Herb Norry, "Farming as a Business" in Farming and the Rural Community in Ontario, T. Fuller, ed., Foundation for Rural Living, Toronto, 1985, p. 81

28. New Scientist, Dec. 17, 1988, (Britain, weekly)

29. Interview, 1986

30. Doyle, p. 174

31. Globe and Mail, Feb. 29, 1988

32. Doyle, p. 176

33. Marc Lappé, Broken Code, the Exploitation of DNA, Sierra Club, 1984, p. 139; and, Omar Sattaur, "Native is Beautiful", New Scientist, June 2, 1988

34. Vandana Shiva, interview, 1986

35. Tom Murphy, "The Structural Transformation of New Brunswick Agriculture, 1951-1981", thesis, University of New Brunswick, 1983

36. Goodman, Sorj and Wilkinson, From Farming to Biotechnology, Basil Blackwell, 1987, p. 34

37. Ibid., p. 138

38. Goodman, et al., describe the transformation of agriculture in terms of what they call "substitutionism" and "appropriationism", the former applying to the output side of agricultural production and the latter to the input side:

Appropriationism: "the discontinuous but persistent undermining of discrete elements of the agricultural production process, their transformation into industrial activities, and their re-incorporation into agriculture as inputs." (p.2)

Substitutionism: "the industrial transformation of agriculture . . . through a series of partial, discontinuous appropriations of the rural labour and biological production processes (machines, fertilizers, hybrid seeds, fine chemicals, biotechnologies), and the parallel development of industrial substitutes for rural products." (p. 2)

The essential first step of substitutionism in the food industry was to interpose mechanized industrial processing and manufacture between the source of field production and final consumption. Once this step had been taken, the rural form of the commodity and its constituents could then be modified and obscured, facilitating its treatment and presentation as an industrial product. (p. 60)

To illustrate: Goodman, et al., describe margarine as "the precursor of industrially fabricated foods" to illustrate this process of substitutionism. Margarine represents "the manufacture of an industrial substitute for a processed *rural* product, butter, using cheaper raw materials." (p. 69)

39. Canadian Agriculture in the Seventies, Report of the Federal Task Force on Agriculture, December 1969, Ottawa, p.9

40. Farm Survey 1988, Farm Credit Corporation, Ottawa, p. 23

41. Canadian Grocer, Dec. 1988

42. Ibid.

43. Farm and Country, May 12, 1987 (weekly, Toronto)

44. Langdon Winner, Autonomous Technology, M.I.T. Press, 1977, and Langdon Winner, The Whale and the Reactor, Univ. of Chicago Press, 1986

45. Researchers at Britain's University of Bristol veterinary school are to receive almost £250,000 from Britain's Ministry of Defence. For some years the Agricultural and Food Research Council has supported work on airborne pathogens that cause disease in farm animals. Despite the fact that it had led to practical improvements in livestock housing, the council decided to drop its funding of the research. The researchers rewrote the grant application and sent it to the Ministry of Defence.

"The project funded by the Ministry of Defence focuses on a single species of bacterium . . . which can cause pneumonia and even death in humans but is not an important pathogen in livestock." Two tenured staff have resigned in protest against the application and its funding and a number of the staff drafted a report explaining the potential military significance of the proposed research. One of the authors explained: "Scientists are now being coerced to subtly alter the direction of their research in an attempt to find funding from the Ministry of Defence since other funds have been withdrawn from them." New Scientist, Dec. 3, 1988

46. Doyle, p. 222

47. Technical Manager, NutraSweet Co.

48. Science, Nov. 11, 1988

49. David Ehrenfeld, "Beyond the Farming Crisis", Technology Review, July, 1987, p. 56

50. Canadian Grocer, Nov. 1988

51. Ibid.

52. Goodman, et al., p. 47-8

53. Globe and Mail, June 13, 1987

54. Bent, Schwaab, Conlin and Jeffery, Intellectual Property Rights in Biotechnology Worldwide, Stockton Press, 1987, p. 141

55. Ibid., p. 139

56. Ibid., p. 167

57. Total agricultural exports for Canada in 1987 were $8.89-billion, of which grains accounted for $3.78-b and red meats for $1.06-b. Total agricultural imports were $6.77-billion, of which fruits and nuts accounted for $1.65-billion; plantation crops, $.84-b; and vegetables, excluding potatoes, $.82-b. Imports of tropical products, mainly from developing countries, totalled $1.27-b in 1987, while the U.S. accounted for 57% of Canada's "agrifood" imports, mostly fruits and vegetables. The net trade surplus for the *food industry* in 1987 was $969-m, but if fish products are excluded, the trade deficit would have been $750-m. Food Market Commentary, Dec. 1988

58. It is not possible to give comparative or even individual figures for these corporations because some of them are privately held and all of them are so complex that meaningful figures are almost impossible to obtain.

59. "Greek and medieval Christian thinkers . . . philosophized about the *oikonomia*, that is, the problem of organizing the *oikos* or household, the

community of those who cooperate under one roof. In Roman law the household, under the "father of the family", was the cell of social life, and the higher and more inclusive organizations both in ancient and medieval life were conceived on the analogy of the household." – E. Heimann, History of Economic Doctrines, Oxford, 1964, p. 22

60. The World Commission on Environment and Development, often referred to as The Brundtland Commission after its Chairman [sic] Gro Harlem Brundtland of Norway, issued its report, Our Common Future in 1987.

61. Quoted in R. Heilbroner, The Essential Adam Smith, Norton, 1986, p. 265

62. Ibid., p. 294

63. Ibid., p. 297

64. UNICEF, The Status of the World's Children 1989, p. 15

65. Ibid., p. 1

66. Karl Polanyi, The Great Transformation, Beacon Press, 1957, p. 117

67. E. Yoxen, The Gene Business, Harper and Row, 1983, p. 142

68. in Heilbroner, p. 322

69. Food 2000 - Global Policies for Sustainable Agriculture, Zed Books, 1987, p. 6

70. Globe and Mail, Jan. 2, 1989

71. R. Levins and R. Lewontin, The Dialectical Biologist, Harvard, 1985, p. 2

72. Kempton Matte, interview, May 1987

73. Goodman, et al., p. 96

74. Ibid., p. 138

75. Doyle, p. 134

76. R. Lewontin, S. Rose and L. Kamin, Not In Our Genes, Pantheon, 1987, p. 167

77. Omar Sattaur, "Native is Beautiful", New Scientist, June 2, 1988

78. Telephone interview, Pesticides Directorate, Agriculture Canada, Jan. 1989

79. Corporate promotion, 1985, and interview with R. Hurnanen, 1988

80. Goodman, et al., p. 51

81. Shaver press release, April 19, 1988

82. Winner, 1986, p. 5

83. Robt. Young, Darwin's Metaphor, Cambridge, 1895, p. 191

84. Ibid., p. 240

85. Walter Anderson, To Govern Evolution, Harcourt Brace Jovanivitch, 1987, p. 56

86. Lewontin, et al., p. 236

87. Paul Davies, "The Creative Cosmos", New Scientist, Dec. 17, 1987

87. Science, May 6, 1988

88. Levins and Lewontin, p. 24

89. Globe and Mail, Sept. 1, 1988

90. UNICEF, p. 30

91. Alan Rayner, "Life in a Collective: Lessons from the Fungi", New Scientist, Nov. 19, 1988

92. Barry Commoner, Science for the People, March/April 1987

93. On a trip through the countryside of western Czechoslovakia I was struck by the realization that the towns and villages were pretty much as they had been for three or four hundred years (the Czech lands were largely spared the destruction of W.W. II) and that the people had always lived in the towns and worked the surrounding farmland. Working the land and owning the land have always been separate issues. The farmers, farm labourers, and peasants of Czechoslovakia have probably never owned the land they worked in the sense we tend to think of, though they may always have had their own garden plots and family animals. If the majority of the land was not owned by the king, then it might have been owned by a feudal lord, the church, the state, or a cooperative, but not likely the farmer who worked it.

94. Lewis Hyde, The Gift, Vintage, 1983, p. 121

95. Colin A. M. Duncan, "Lessons in Sustainability from English History" in Global Perspectives on Agroecology and Sustainable Agricultural Systems, edited by D. van Dusan and P. Allan, Univ. of Calfornia Press, 1988 (in press)

BIBLIOGRAPHY

Anderson, Walter T.: <u>To Govern Evolution</u>, Harcourt Brace Jovanovich, Boston, 1987

Barber, Clarence, commissioner: <u>Report of the Royal Commission on Farm Machinery</u>, Information Canada, Ottawa, 1971,

Bennett, Jon, with George, Susan: <u>The Hunger Machine</u>, CBC, Toronto, 1987

<u>Canadian Agriculture in the Seventies</u>, Report of the Federal Task Force on Agriculture, December 1969, Ottawa, 475pp.

<u>Canadian Grocer</u>, Maclean Hunter, Toronto, monthly

Cronon, Wm: <u>Changes in the Land - Indians, Colonists, and the Ecology of New England</u>, Hill and Wang, New York, 1983

<u>Development Dialogue</u>, 1988: 1 – 2, Cary Fowler, Eva Lachkovics, Pat Mooney and Hope Shand, "The Laws of Life – Another Development and the New Biotechnologies", published by the Dag Hammarskjold Foundation, Uppsala, Sweden

Doyle, Jack: <u>Altered Harvest - Agriculture, Genetics, and the Fate of the World's Food Supply</u>, Viking, New York, 1985

<u>Food 2000 - Global Policies for Sustainable Agriculture</u>, Report to the World Commission on Environment and Development, Zed Books, 1987

<u>Food in Canada</u>, Maclean Hunter, Toronto, monthly

<u>Food Market Commentary</u>, Agriculture Canada, Ottawa, quarterly

Fukuoka, Masanobu: <u>One Straw Revolution</u>, Bantam New Age, 1985, (Chapters 1-3)

George, Susan, and Paige, Nigel: <u>Food for Beginners</u>, Writers and Readers Publishing Cooperative, London, 1982

George, Susan: <u>Ill Fares the Land - Essays on Food, Hunger, and Power</u>, Institute for Policy Studies, Washington, 1984

Giangrande, Carole: <u>Down to Earth - The Crisis in Canadian Farming</u>, Anansi, Toronto, 1985

Goodman, Sorj, & Wilkinson: From Farming to Biotechnology, Basil Blackwell, Oxford, 1987

Heilbroner, Robert L.: The Essential Adam Smith, Norton, 1986

Hyde, Lewis: The Gift: Imagination and the Erotic Life of Property, Vintage Books, 1983, (Part One, "A Theory of Gifts")

Kenny, Martin: Biotechnology: The University-Industrial Complex, Yale University Press, New Haven, 1986

Kloppenburg, J.R., Ed: Seeds and Sovereignty - The Use and Contol of Plant Genetic Resources, Duke University Press, 1988

Kramer, Mark: Three Farms - Making Milk, Meat and Money from the American Soil, Bantam 1981, Harvard 1987

Lappé, Marc: Broken Code; the Exploitation of DNA, Sierra Club, San Francisco, 1984

Levins, Richard, & Lewontin, Richard: The Dialectical Biologist, Harvard University Press, Cambridge, Mass., 1985

Lewontin, R.C., Rose, S., and Kamin, Leon: Not In Our Genes, Biology, Ideology, and Human Nature; Pantheon Books, New York, 1984

Morgan, Dan: Merchants of Grain, Penguin, 1980

New Scientist, IPC Magazines, Britain, weekly

Pacey, Arnold: The Culture of Technology, MIT Press, Cambridge, 1983

Ram's Horn, The, (14 Blong Ave., Toronto, Canada M4M 1P2)

Schell, Orville: Modern Meat, Vintage, 1985

UNICEF: The State of the World's Children 1989, Oxford University Press, 1989

Warnock, John W.: The Politics of Hunger, Methuen, 1987

Winner, Langdon: The Whale and the Reactor, A Search for Limits in an Era of High Technology, Univ. of Chicago Press, 1986

Winner, Langdon: Autonomous Technology, MIT Press, Cambridge, 1977

Young, Robert M.: Darwin's Metaphor, Nature's Place in Victorian Culture, Cambridge Univ. Press, Cambridge, 1985

Yoxen, Edward: The Gene Business, Who Should Control Biology?, Harper and Row, New York, 1983

INDEX